CAPTAIN ON THE YANGTZE

THE MEMOIRS OF A EUROPEAN SKIPPER ON CHINA'S YANGTZE RIVER

PETER MENDER

TRANSLATED BY HILLAR KALMAR

EARNSHAW
BOOKS

Captain on the Yangtze

By Peter Mender

ISBN-13: 978-988-8769-09-4

HISTORY / ASIA / CHINA

EB150

Published by Earnshaw Books Ltd. (Hong Kong)

To my parents with deep gratitude for their
unconditional love and guidance in life.

Chinese place names in this book use their Wade-Giles spellings, as written by Mender. For most of the 20th Century, the Wade-Giles system was the standard method of Romanizing, or transcribing, Chinese (Mandarin) language characters to English. To make places easier to locate on modern maps, the current Hanyu Pinyin Romanized name is shown where appropriate, but only after the first use of the Wade-Giles name.

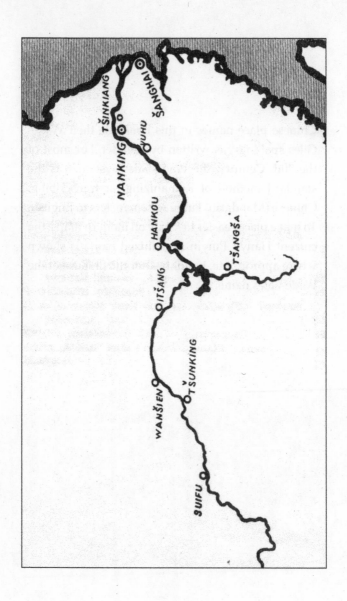

Contents

CAPTAIN ON THE YANGTZE

PREFACE

BY HILLAR KALMAR

Peter Mender and Johann Kalmar, my grandfather, were first cousins. They were born a year apart to sisters in the early 1880s. Both grew up on Baltic Sea islands and became Master Mariners, qualified to command all ships on all seas. Mender and Kalmar each started their careers as deck-boys aboard wooden sailing ships, which eventually led to captaining steamships in the Far East.

I recall Peter Mender's name from a young age. I knew he was highly respected from the way my father spoke about him in stories about Estonia and China, where my father's family had lived during the 1920s and 1930s while his father worked for Möller & Co. out of Shanghai.

In 2009, I learned that after Mender's 1938 retirement from Standard Oil, as the longest serving captain on the Upper Yangtze River, he had returned to Estonia and written his memoirs. These were published in 1940 in Tallinn, Estonia under the title "*Kolmkümmend Aastat Meremehena Kaug-Idas.*" I had just finished compiling a family tree and had connected with distant cousins. Mender had been their grandfather and although they had a copy of his book in safe deposit, they were unable to read Estonian.

I translated Mender's book for his relatives, and anyone else with an interest in his account of life along China's Yangtze River during the early 20th Century. If there are any inaccuracies in translation these are solely my responsibility.

In addition to Mender and Kalmar, over a dozen Estonian

shipmasters worked in the Far East at the time. One of these was another relative, Capt. Siim Roos, who married Mender's sister. The Roos and Kalmar families shared a home in Shanghai. Roos occasionally worked on Standard Oil vessels in China, sometimes as mate while Mender was Master, and my father was certain that most photos in Mender's book were taken by Roos, who apparently always carried a camera. After leaving Shanghai, all three men worked for an Estonian shipping firm named Merilaid & Co. of which they were founding shareholders.

Master, Captain or Skipper are synonymous terms denoting a licensed mariner in ultimate command of a ship. A person with such a designation is responsible for all of a ship's operations, including navigation, crew management, cargo and compliance with all laws and regulations including immigration and customs. An unlimited Master's license allows the captain to operate any vessel worldwide and requires many years of seagoing experience as a third mate/officer, a second mate/ officer, and as chief mate or first officer. A Master at sea has other official authorities including: the safety and security of the crew and passengers; acting as a notary or as the police; and the use of deadly force in cases of mutiny, assault by pirates, defending the interests of the flag state and the ship's owners and cargo owners, etc. While a ship is at sea the captain is the supreme authority, and that is the authority that Mender bore for more than three decades.

Estonia is one of nine nations bordering the Baltic Sea. The others are Germany, Denmark, Sweden, Finland, Russia, Latvia, Lithuania and Poland. From the end of the Great Northern War through World War I, half of these countries were under Russian rule.

Peter Mender was born Peter Julius Aleksander Mender on February 21, 1883 to Peter Reedik Mender and Emma Lisette

All, the second-oldest of eight siblings. The family farm, on the island of Vilsandi, Estonia, is now part of Vilsandi National Park. The family name was originally Mänder and became anglicized to Mender.

Before moving to China, Mender worked in Vladivostok for a steamship line owned by a Baltic German Count named Heinrich Hugovitch Keyserling. Keyserling started his shipping line in 1906 after serving as an Imperial Russian naval officer and then establishing a whaling fleet, which was confiscated by the Japanese during the 1904 Russo-Japanese war. While working for Keyerling, Mender hired a crewman who other captains shunned. Being a sailor was physically and mentally demanding work and some masters and officers treated their crewmen harshly. The crewman Mender mentions, a sailor named Jaan Umb, was badly treated until he snapped, killing his tormentors, in what is known as the 1887 *Johannes* Tragedy. Afterwards other captains would not hire this man. Mender writes that Umb had been his best hand and when Umb quit to find other work, Mender wrote him a favorable recommendation.

Almost 4,000 miles long, the Yangtze River is the world's third longest after the Nile and the Amazon rivers. It also features the world's most populous watershed. Prior to completion of the Three Gorges Dam, the Yangtze River underwent seasonal flooding that affected many millions of people. As Mender writes, floods in the early 1930s were particularly bad, many people drowned, crops were ruined and famine ensued. The Three Gorges Dam reservoir has covered many, but not all, of the villages, towns, rapids, gorges and navigation markers that Mender writes about, obscuring the great difficulty that vessels had in transiting the treacherous Upper Yangtze River.

In 1900, Captain Samuel Cornell Plant, an Englishman, was the first person to take a steamship all the way to Chungking along the Upper River without the use of trackers. Previously, junks and all other vessels navigating the Upper River were pulled upstream over the rapids and shoals, against the current, by men called trackers. These laborers were beasts of burden who wore slings around their bodies that were tied to hemp or bamboo ropes, or wires, to collectively heave vessels upstream while they rhythmically chanted and slowly moved ahead. Most trackers were barefoot and wore little, if any, clothing. They shuffled along paths worn into rock by previous generations of trackers while hunched over and straining greatly. Many accidentally fell to their deaths from cliff walls. There were tens of thousands if not hundreds of thousands of trackers along the Upper River. Trackers were very poor and their hazardous and physically demanding work meant a short life, which averaged about five years after they started. Their income was barely adequate to support life and researchers considered their lives to be worse than those of Negro slaves prior to the American Civil War.

Captain Plant later entered the Chinese Imperial Maritime Customs Service and became Senior Inspector, Upper Yangtze River. In 1920 the Service published the handbook Plant had written to guide shipmasters in navigating the Upper River. This remarkable book provides detailed maps and names for all rocks, whirlpools and shoals of interest to shipmasters, including techniques for mooring and safe passage. It is highly likely that Mender had a copy of this handbook.

The Chinese Maritime Customs Service was founded 1854 in Shanghai as an information dissemination and tax collection agency. It was one of the world's first bureaucracies and operated for almost one hundred years, collecting significant revenue for the Chinese central government. The Service was highly organized and efficient and corruption was virtually non-existent at least until 1929 when China became responsible for setting the tariff and rates increased from about 5% to more than 30%. Foreigners working for the Customs Service helped to spread knowledge about China across the world. In the 1920s virtually all Chinese trade was controlled by the Service and it collected about one third of all tax revenue available to Beijing.

There are numerous books that describe life in China between the end of the last imperial dynasty in 1912, the Qing dynasty, and creation of the People's Republic of China in 1949. This almost forty-year period of fighting between regional warlords, the Nationalist government and Communist fighters to bring the large country under centralized government was complicated by Japan's invasion of China. From the Warlord Era (1916-1928) through to the Second Sino-Japanese War (1937-1945), Mender continued to work on the Yangtze River for Standard Oil.

Commercial interests from other countries were drawn to China by the country's vast population and resources. By the end of the mid-19th Century, following opium wars and other confrontations, treaties between China and other nations granted the Western powers and Japan a long list of territorial concessions. Construction and manufacturing soon followed, trade started to flourish and other Western nations soon arrived as well.

At least initially, Mender was likely directly employed by a Standard Oil subsidiary company operating in China called Socony River and Coastal Fleet. Standard Oil Company was founded in 1870 by the Rockefellers and was a predecessor of today's ExxonMobil Corporation. At the time, it was the world's dominant oil company and one of the world's first and largest multinational corporations. Standard Oil operated under a trust structure until 1911, when the U.S. government broke the Trust up into dozens of smaller companies because of its monopolistic business practices. Two companies that had been within the Standard Oil Trust were Standard Oil Company of New York ("Socony") and the Vacuum Oil Company. In 1931 these companies merged to create The Socony-Vacuum Oil Company. In 1933 Socony-Vacuum entered a joint venture with Standard Oil Company of New Jersey, or Jersey Standard, to create The Standard-Vacuum Oil Company ("Stanvac") which combined Vacuum's focus on lubricating oils and their Asian distribution system with Socony's production and refining operations.

Mender's use of the term 'Chinaman' in his memoirs conforms to its historical usage and is not derogative in any sense. Chinaman is an English word that denotes a person of Chinese ethnicity and sometimes is an indiscriminate term for a person of East Asia. Similar usage occurred with terms such as Frenchman, Dutchman, Irishman etc. and these generally remain unobjectionable in their usage today however, modern dictionaries typically describe the term Chinaman as derogatory and today its use is limited.

Prior to Pearl Harbor, Stanvac was the largest single direct U.S. investment in East Asia. Standard Oil's U.S. production capacity exceeded domestic market demand in the late 1800's, and the Company began looking at export markets. Due to China's large population and the opportunity to displace vegetable oils as a fuel for lamps, Standard Oil began marketing kerosene there during the 1890's and promoted its advantages as being longer burning with less smell and smoke. This resulted in the slogan "Oil for the lamps of China" that was popular among American businessman at the time. The slogan became the title of a novel written by the wife of an oil executive, about which a movie was made in 1935. Chinese response to kerosene was positive and soon China became Standard Oil's largest Asian market. As its trademark and brand in China, Standard Oil adopted the name "Meifu" in Chinese characters and "Mei Foo" in roman letters. The character for "Mei" means "beautiful", and the name Mei Foo translated as "beautiful confidence" or "beautiful and trustworthy". Mei Foo became the name for the tin lamp that Standard Oil made and sold cheaply or gave away to Chinese peasants, encouraging them to change lighting fuel from vegetable oils to kerosene. The slogan "Oil for the lamps of China" effectively meant that if you gave people a lamp then chances were that they would buy the kerosene from you.

Stanvac operated a North China Division from Shanghai that operated hundreds of river-going vessels including motor barges, steamers, launches, tankers and tugboats. To distribute its products, Standard Oil built storage tanks, canneries, warehouses and offices in key Chinese cities. The canneries packaged bulk oil from ocean tankers into five-gallon tins. Up to thirteen tankers operated on the Yangtze River, the largest of which were *Mei Ping* (1,108 gross tons), meaning "Beautiful Tranquility", *Mei Hsia* (1,048 gt) meaning "Beautiful Gorges" and *Mei An* (934 gt). The tankers had multiple holds to carry bulk oils, cargo holds for packaged oils and bulletproof wheelhouses to provide protection from bandits.

Mei An was launched in 1901 and was the first vessel in the Standard Oil fleet. Other vessels included *Mei Chuen, Mei Foo, Mei Hung, Mei Kiang, Mei Lu, Mei Tan, Mei Su, Mei Xia, Mei Ying,* and *Mei Yun. Mei Hsia,* a tanker, was specially designed for river duty and was built by New Engineering and Shipbuilding Works of Shanghai, who also built the 500 ton launch *Mei Foo* in 1912. *Mei Hsia* was launched in 1926 and carried 350 tons of bulk oil in three holds, plus a forward cargo hold and space between decks for carrying general cargo or packed oil. She had a length of 206 ft., a beam of 32 ft., depth of 10 ft. 6 in. and a bulletproof wheelhouse. *Mei Ping* ("Beautiful Tranquility") launched in 1927, was designed offshore but assembled and finished in Shanghai. Her oil fuel burners came from the U.S. and her water tube boilers came from England.

Bandits, both men and women, roamed outside China's main towns and cities in large groups, stealing whatever they could to survive. Most had been farmers or other law-abiding citizens before floods destroyed Yangtze basin crops, resulting in famine. Any remaining food was commandeered by regional armies, leaving the peasants to choose between starvation, cannibalism or banditry as there was no government to help them. The third option was the most popular and the survival instinct led people to theft, murder, kidnapping and ransom. Defeated soldiers from warlord armies were also starving and often joined the bandits, bringing their guns. The number of bandits peaked around 1930 when they were believed to number more than 500,000.

The establishment of foreign owned businesses in China was accompanied by Britain, Germany, America, France and other nations sending warships to protect their commercial interests in the Yangtze River basin. American naval forces operated in China from the late 19th century through World War II. Initially, America used four vessels acquired from the Philippines that had been confiscated during the Spanish-American War but these could not navigate above Ichang. In 1913, two purpose built gunboats, USS *Palos* and USS *Monocacy*, were shipped from California to China and then, in the 1920s, six more gunboats were built in Shanghai, three pairs of sister ships of different sizes – USS *Luzon* and *Mindanao*, USS *Oahu and Panay*, and USS *Guam* and *Tutuila* which were the smallest. All were able to reach Chungking. The Yangtze River Patrol or YangPat officially became part of the U.S. Asiatic Fleet in 1921 and patrolled the Yangtze River up to 1,000 miles from the ocean. The fleet's purpose was to protect U.S. missionaries and business interests in China. Treaty ports were places where foreigners were permitted to live and conduct business while under the laws of their own country and not of China.

The Standard Oil tankers commanded by Mender were often under the protection of American gunboats while on the river, particularly during times of bandit uprisings and skirmishes between warlords, when armed marines would also be ordered onto the tank ships. The 1966 movie, "The Sand Pebbles," starring Steve McQueen and Candice Bergen, portrayed a fictional gunboat named the USS *San Pablo* to re-enact what foreign merchant ships faced on the Yangtze River during the turbulent mid-1920s time of China's "awakening" when life became engulfed by revolution.

In mid-1926 Chiang Kai-shek became Commander-in-Chief of the National Revolutionary Army and immediately launched a military campaign known as the Northern Expedition, with the objective of defeating the warlords controlling northern China and of unifying the country under the Kuomintang organization, or KMT, whose ultimate goal was democracy. The KMT had strong socialist elements and ties with Chinese communists and Soviet agents, which Chiang believed threatened his control over KMT. In early 1927 he began a purge of communists and suspected dissidents, with tens of thousands killed and driven from urban centers. Chiang's expulsion of the communists and their Soviet advisers led to the beginning of the Chinese Civil War, which ended, for a while, in 1928 when Chiang achieved control over all of China. During this so-called 1928-1937 Republican Era, many features of a modern, functional Chinese state were developed. Some aspects of foreign imperialism, concessions and privileges were moderated through diplomacy during this time period. The government also moved to modernize the legal and penal systems, attempted to stabilize prices, amortize debts, reform the banking and currency systems, build railroads and highways, improve public health facilities, legislate against narcotics and increase industrial and agricultural production. Narcotics were an issue because in the early 1900s opium was legal in China and with more than 12 million opium addicts nearly 30 percent of adult males were addicted. The 1909 Shanghai Opium Commission had been created to deal with this issue, which led to The 1911 Hague Opium Conference and then to The Hague Opium Convention in 1912 however no international mechanisms were agreed to and narcotic control remained within each nation's domestic legislation.

Progress was also made in furthering education and the so-called New Life Movement was launched to promote moral values and personal discipline. Mandarin was promoted as a standard tongue and the establishment of communication facilities, including radio, were used to encourage a sense of Chinese Nationalism that previously had not been possible due to the nation's fractured status.

Successes made by the Nationalists, however, were met with constant political and military upheavals. While urban areas were now generally under KMT's control, the countryside remained under the influence of weakened yet undefeated warlords and Communists. Chiang often resolved issues of warlord obstinacy through military action, such as the Central Plains War, which almost bankrupted the government and caused many casualties. In 1931, Hu Han-min, Chiang's old supporter, publicly voiced concern that Chiang Kai-shek's position as both premier and president flew in the face of the democratic ideals of the Nationalist government. Chiang had Hu put under house arrest but he was released after national condemnation, and went on to establish a rival government in Guangzhou. The split resulted in military campaigns between Hu's Canton Government and its supporters, and Chiang's Nationalist Government. Chiang only prevailed due to a shift in allegiance by the warlord Chang Hsueh-liang, who had previously supported Hu Han-min.

Throughout his rule, eradication of the Communist Party of China, which had been founded in 1921, remained Chiang's dream. Having regrouped and established a Chinese Soviet Republic, Chiang led his armies against them. With help from foreign military advisers, Chiang's Fifth Campaign finally surrounded the Red Army in 1934. The Communists, tipped-off that a Nationalist offensive was coming, retreated as part of the Long March, which saw Mao Zedong rise from a mere military official to the practical leader of the Chinese Communist Party. After many other battles, including another Sino-Japanese War, the Communists defeated the KMT and came to rule all of mainland China in 1949, thus bringing an end to the Chinese Civil War.

Prior to World War II, Japan was the dominant manufacturing, economic and military power in East Asia. Japan continuously sought to expand its area of influence and control, especially coveting resource rich areas in the Russian Far East, Manchuria and Korea. Japan decisively defeated Russia in the 1904 Russo-Japanese War, and in the following years targeted China. Mender's memoirs highlight incidents with the Japan military including one in 1932, and the 1937 "Bloody Sunday" when China tried to attack a Japanese naval vessel near Shanghai's Bund but accidentally bombed its own citizens.

The decades-long regional turmoil reached a peak in December 1937 when Japan attacked Nanking. The terrible attacks on the people of that city were witnessed by foreigners aboard merchant ships in their gunboat-led convoys. Japanese boldness had grown over the years and during their attack on Nanking, Japanese warplanes bombed foreign ships on the Yangtze, sinking the gunboat USS *Panay* along with three Standard Oil vessels, one of which was captained by Mender. The Panay Incident, as it became known, was Japan's first direct attack against foreign assets in China. Previously, the fighting that took place between Chinese and Japanese forces strove to avoid foreign vessels, assets and citizens as they did not want foreign powers to intervene.

After being attacked by Japanese warplanes on December 12, 1937, the U.S.S. *Panay* sank approximately 28 miles upriver from Nanking. At the time of the attack she had just evacuated the final U.S. embassy staff from Nanking and with these individuals aboard she began escorting three Standard Oil ships (*Mei Ping, Mei An and Mei Hsia*) and 14 small barges upriver. The 3 tankers, each larger than the *Panay*, carried approximately 800 Chinese employees and their families. There were two movie photographers aboard *Panay* at the time she was bombed, Norman Alley of Universal and Eric Mayell of Fox Movietone. Both cameramen filmed as much as they could during the incident and each firm produced a newsreel. The Japanese planes that dived and attacked the convoy were biplanes.

Mender's ship, the *Mei Hsia*, was also struck by bombs and sunk during the Panay Incident. Mender, along with the other captains and foreign nationals, including foreign reporters and film crews, helped to save as many people as possible no matter their nationality. For their help in rescuing survivors of the Panay Incident, the U.S. Secretary of the Navy awarded the Navy Expeditionary Medal to various naval personnel and civilians, including Captain Mender.

During the 1946 Tokyo War Crimes Trial, Colonel Hashimoto was one of 28 Japanese leaders indicted for "plotting to rule the world" and charged with 55 war crimes. Hashimoto had been a member of a group working to control the Japanese government since at least 1931, the year that Japan invaded Manchuria.

Standard Oil had a mandatory retirement age of fifty-five for ship captains. Mender reached this age in early 1938 and returned to Estonia, started to receive his pension and wrote his memoirs, which were published in 1940. Mender's memoirs of working as a captain in the Russian Far East and China are remarkable as they provide a fascinating first-hand account of life in that part of the world in the early 20th century that is much more vivid than documents woven together by historians years later.

Mender and three other captains, including his youngest brother Johannes, established the Estonian shipping company Merilaid & Co. in 1930. At the start of World War II Merilaid owned four vessels, the steamships *Merisaar, Naissaar, Osmussaar* and *Kuressaar*. The *Osmussaar* was expropriated by the Soviets in 1942. The *Merisaar* was sunk by German aircraft in the Bay of Biscay in 1940. The *Naissaar* was also expropriated and sank on August 29, 1941 after striking a mine while part of a Soviet convoy from Tallinn to St. Petersburg (Leningrad). The SS *Kuressaar*, meanwhile, was at sea when Russia moved to nationalize the remaining assets of the company. By the time the ship arrived in Baltimore, Estonia's New York Consul, anticipating false Soviet claims, had already transferred title to a newly created Honduras shipping firm called Estoduras. Soviet claims were eventually rejected by the court and Mender along with a son-in-law managed the ship under a new name until it was sold.

Hillar Kalmar
Vancouver, October 2021

1

VOYAGES AS A SAILOR

I COME FROM an old Vilsandi Island seafaring family, so it was fitting that I started my own maritime life at age seven.[1] I spent my summers working aboard coastal sailboats and went to school during the winters, and at age fifteen, I began working on ocean-going vessels. At age eighteen, I left my father's sailboat *Taavet* in England and began working aboard cargo ships to various countries.

Initially, I happened to join a Norwegian steamer, *Farmand*, on which, in addition to visiting harbors in the Baltic Sea, I also traveled to ports on the Danube River and the Black Sea. When I left this ship in 1902 there were awesome battles going on between the British and the Boers in South Africa. I was so inspired by the Boers' valiant resistance against British efforts

---

1   Vilsandi is a small Estonian island northwest of the large island of Saaremaa

to subjugate them that I intended to go and volunteer to help the Boers. This intention resulted in my joining *Clen Grand,* a British barque, as senior seaman. The ship was going to Port Elisabeth, South Africa, where I planned to leave her. The ship was large, 741 tons, and the crew consisted of many nationalities. The captain and second officer were Irish, the first officer was Scottish and others were French, Norwegian and Portuguese, with one American and even one Finn. The cargo was coal.

The voyage from England began at night during a snowstorm. The men had been tippling the prior evening and all were inebriated.

During the night the second officer sent me to gather the foresails and ordered three of us onto the yardarm. Two men went to the downwind side, fastened the sails there and went back down. I, however, was alone on the upwind side. With the strong storm most of the sails had been blown to the side I was on, which made securing the sails very difficult and, on top of this, the bracket holding the rope I was standing on broke, as it was rusted through. I was about to fall when I instinctively grabbed the yardarm and managed to stay up. As it was impossible for me to single-handedly pull the sail onto the yardarm and secure it, I fastened the sail where it was as best as I could, and climbed down. There, the second officer cursed me and asked what was happening up there and said the sail was poorly tied. I tried to explain, however I didn't speak English well enough and all I could communicate over the officer's shouts was that things topside were "all right."

In the morning, the second officer himself climbed the mast and saw that the bracket was broken. He came down spitting and shaking his head, clasped me on the back with happiness and said I was "all right". If I had fallen off the mast during the night, the responsibility would have been his. A few days later, after we passed through the Bay of Biscay, a strong headwind arose, the waves grew large and the ship began to roll strongly, resulting in broken sail lines. We worked for ten days in this storm and all we could do was to keep fixing new sail lines and as soon as we were able to fasten one, others broke and except for keeping only two men on watch, the entire crew was on duty, standing in water the whole time. At times, the waves were so large they washed over the cabin and everything was wet and cold, however the ship's hull withstood the storm. To this day, I'm amazed the masts didn't break. After this storm, we had good weather until we reached South Africa.

The trade winds were blowing and the trip took 93 days. The ship was managed according to British laws, including the rations, which were barely sufficient to sustain life. We were given poor quality, fatty, salted meat several times each week and also some unsalted meat. Because bread gets moldy within a day in the tropics, it needs to be made every day. On our ship so much bread was made at a time that we often ate moldy bread. There were worms in the flour and groats. Lemon juice was provided to mix with the drinking water. Although the food was poor, the rules were so strict that we could not openly complain.

The crew mostly got along fine. Of course there were fights, especially as the men were of so many different nationalities. I was always believed to be a Russian, and was cursed and asked why I didn't eat candles and drink fat, as there seemed to be a general belief that this is what Russians ate. As I was relatively big, strong, and young, I was always able to fend for myself. After a while, when the crew was more familiar with each other, the weaker members knew who they were and usually gave up their positions, and fights were less common. The Norwegian, who beat everyone up, was the "cock of the sailors' quarters." Disagreements come easily when people live together at sea for three months, and some foreigners are quite sensitive about their heritage. The ship's officers did not get involved in any disputes among the crew.

We made it to Africa, to Port Elizabeth in Algoa Bay. This is an open bay with no shelter against storms from the southeast, the south, or the southwest. Thus, ships used two anchors and, in addition, when a storm approached, hemp ropes 200 fathoms long and eight inches thick were brought from shore and dropped in with the anchors.

We spent 2½ months unloading there. When the weather was favorable, the barge came alongside the ship, bags were filled with coal and heaved onto the barge, and a tug took the barge back to shore. Sometimes storms lasted four or five days and did not allow for any unloading, and we lived through several of these. The waves were so large that we were thrown out of our hammocks during the night. There was a wharf that small ships could tie up to during the day. However, we were anchored offshore, and during our stay only the captain and officers were allowed ashore.

Due to the war,[2] many ships were there with war materials. Out of interest, one day I counted 43 inactive ships at anchor, the smallest of which was Swedish, 57 ocean trampers either loading or unloading, and some steamers and other ships.

My youthful eagerness for adventure had me convinced to jump ship and join the war to help the Boers, whom the British were oppressing and taking land from by force. This was the reason I had left home. However, there were no opportunities to jump ship as we were two miles offshore, we were not allowed to put dinghies into the ocean, and sharks prevented the possibility of swimming ashore. Seven men from an American sailboat tried

---

2   The Boer War, 1899-1902

to swim to shore, but only one made it and the other six fell prey to the sharks. The largest ships were anchored as far as five miles offshore.

The Boer War ended when we had almost finished unloading. Most of the battles were inland and out of our sight. There were not any Boers to be seen around Port Elizabeth. However, we did see some Kaffirs or Hottentots who seemed like a vastly underdeveloped people and whose voices were very harsh on the ears and sounded like abominable shouting. They were hardworking however, and managed pretty well with unloading the bags of coal, and they didn't have it in them to disobey white men.

After our 2½ months in the Bay we were ordered to Barbados in the West Indies. From there we sailed to Brunswick, in the American state of Georgia, and then to Buenos Aires. In America, we were at anchor for 8½ months without shore leave, except for the captain and officers. When the crew finally got ashore, there was a lot of drinking. The second day after the men had gone ashore, the captain went to bail them out of jail. After being on the ship again for a few days, the entire crew ran off.

The only ones left were the captain, his son, the officers and myself. After the ship was loaded and back at anchor, a new crew was brought onboard. This happened late at night with the crew drunk, as usual, and then the order was given to heave anchor. It was pretty horrible working on the ship in the dark with a drunken crew and only a few clear heads. The night was spent messing around trying to get the ship properly downriver, so it was daybreak by the time we reached the mouth of the river. Thus began our voyage to Buenos Aires. The captain had expected the journey to take two months, but we were at sea for 100 days. We ran short of food during the voyage, and caught dolphins by putting a white rag on the end of a fishing pole and holding it near the surface of the water. The dolphins would jump after the rag and be caught. Dolphin meat is very dry, however, and you would eat it only when starving. We fried the meat in salty animal fat that had been saved from the food stores.

The trade winds brought rain and thus we had fresh water. Nonetheless, water was still rationed — a small barrel every three days for the entire crew.

Three hundred miles from the mouth of the La Plata River, we were hit by a hurricane, called a pombero, which blew for 24 hours. Our sails were fastened, except for one on the rear mast, so the ship's prow would face the wind. Waves wrecked half of the crew's quarters, where fortunately there were no men. Large 18-inch square beams began to move and hit the bulkhead, which began to fall apart. Cracks appeared in the deck and the ship started to leak. No one was injured as the crew had taken shelter on the rear deck. The weather soon improved, although the ship leaked like an old basket and every 15 minutes we had to pump water out for 20 minutes. In addition, it got very hot and though we were starving we had to pump! We sailed up the La Plata River to Buenos Aires. A pilot came aboard and we sailed for seven days in hellishly hot weather, pumping continuously, until we reached Buenos Aires.

The ship was allowed to run aground onto the north bank of the river. Mud filled the cracks and the leaking stopped. The cargo began to be unloaded and then the crew ran away again. They were tired of being hungry. Some of the men were lured away by better job offers, for which they had to pay a fee of two months wages, and they went out to sea again, usually on the next ship to leave.

Everyone was interested in hiring me as well and said I should jump ship, on which I'd already been for 1½ years.

The others had jumped ship and the captain also wanted to be rid of me, because after 1½ years I was owed £50 and he wanted this for himself. However, I wouldn't leave so the captain had me unload the cargo of planks, which took 32 days. The work was very hard but as I was 19 years old and very strong, I was able to manage. The first workday was a Saturday. When I lifted the first plank to my shoulder the weight bowed my feet but I was still able to work the full day. On Sunday, I was so stiff and sore that I was unable to get up. On Monday however, I was able to work again. When I was unloading the planks I received better food than when we had been at sea. After the cargo hold was empty there was an order to return to North America and load more planks. The voyage started with another new crew. The pilot was just about to leave the ship when a storm blew in. In a panic, we were able to drop anchor and secure the sails and then the storm was upon us. This time we were on the river, in the storm, for 14 hours.

The waves washed away the mud filling the cracks in the hull and the ship began to leak again.

The captain wrote to the ship's owners in England that the ship leaked, that it was impossible to carry any more cargo and that he was taking the ship to Barbados to wait for their reply, as it was certain that in its present condition any local authorities would not let the ship load.

After we had been in Barbados for two days there came a reply from the ship's owners that we were to return home, and so we sailed for England.

Before reaching England, I began to show symptoms of scurvy. Fortunately, the voyage went quickly and my symptoms improved with fresh food.

From England I returned to Estonia with plans to enter a maritime school. I had been away for three years and had survived many hardships at sea, and the poor diet had left me so thin that even my own mother did not recognize me at first.

7

2

TO THE FAR EAST!

AFTER STUDYING at the Kuressaare Maritime School in Saaremaa, Estonia, I went to Magnusholm near Riga, Latvia and passed my exam in 1904. For a brief time afterward, I was first officer on a sailing ship, and in the fall I once again sought service on a foreign ship, this time ending up on a British steamship. Subsequently, in 1907, I graduated from the Riga Maritime School as a fully qualified ship's captain. Afterwards, I worked briefly as officer on a steamship based in Liepaja, Latvia.

In St. Petersburg that fall, while looking in vain for a ship to hire me, I ran into a classmate who was planning to leave for Vladivostok the next day. His brother was a ship's captain there and he hoped to find a similar job. I immediately decided to go along and try my luck. I was able to convince my classmate to delay his departure by one day so I could prepare for the journey, and so we traveled together by train to Vladivostok.

After a tiring and difficult 17-day rail trip we arrived in Vladivostok. Within a few days, I was fortunate to be hired by an East Asian shipping company for an officer's position on one of their ships. The vessel *Baltica* was a 3,000-ton ship that carried both passengers and cargo. The ship traveled on a route between China, Japan and Vladivostok. At first, working on this ship was unfamiliar and strange. The crew consisted of Chinese and Russians, and most of the latter were typical cutthroats who had done their time on Sakhalin Island and then had been sent here. On one occasion, the Russians got into a quarrel with local dockworkers in Japan, that might have ended quite badly for them as there were 300 Japanese. However, we were somehow able to quell the trouble without too many consequences, although some men had been roughed up.

After this, when I had been working for a short time on another ship, the 4,000-ton *Asial*, I was sent onboard the ship *Mongolia*, which kept an express route between Vladivostok, Nagasaki and Shanghai. This fast steamship could travel at 18 knots and working conditions onboard were very good, but were extremely tiring and demanding, because we had to keep a strict schedule to ensure there were no delays in mail delivery. This was very difficult, especially during the heavy seasonal storms of the fall and winter.

Russia's Far Eastern coast is mostly mountainous with large forests, particularly in the north. During summer, from mid-April through August, there is almost continuous fog which is the main maritime hazard during this time of year. Summers are warm overall but are humid due to the fog. The winters are cold. The prevailing winds are from the north and snowstorms are frequent.

Indigenous tribes here include the Alutors, the Koryaks and the Kereks. The first two are a rudimentary people who seem

9

marginally evolved and survive by hunting and fishing. The Kereks are physically stronger and their limited needs are met by elk, whose herds they follow around with the seasons. All three of the peoples mentioned are of the yellow Chinese race.

Judging by their names, all of them are of the Russian religion but only in a distant sense as their Russian first names were given to them by priests. Many of these natives wanted to be baptized with the Tsar's name, Nicholas, for which the priests took a substantial fee of one or two sable skins. Receiving their name from a Russian priest was the limit of the natives' encounter with Russian religion and, having had such a whiff, the natives remained their totally pagan selves. They prayed reverently in front of heathen-like straw figures that they themselves had made and dressed in their best rags. For them this was more comforting and easier to understand than the God of their distant emperor Tsar Nicholas II.

In addition to the above-mentioned natives, there were also people from Korea who seemed more highly developed and who engaged in agricultural pursuits and fishing.

I also met a lot of Chinese. Some stayed here only during the summer and returned to China for the winter. They hunted, gathered sea cabbage and worked for the Russians. Many Chinese made their living as thieves and robbers, moving around frequently in large gangs and seizing others' belongings from even the larger villages.

The Tsar's own people, the Russians, were engaged in many things. Some residents had migrated from western parts of Russia to escape persecution for their religious beliefs. Some had come to prospect for gold or to catch fish. Others had formerly been forced laborers who had then been sent here to live. Russians also occupied the various official positions necessary to administer government functions and to carry out related duties.

PETER MENDER

There were also a number of Estonians who had settled on the shores of Amur Bay near Vladivostok and Ussuri Bay. In April 1909, I went on board *Georg*, a ship owned by Count Keyserling, a Baltic-German, as second officer. The Count's ships followed two routes during the summer, one south from Vladivostok as far as Korea, and the other north from Vladivostok to the Russian province of Pri-Amur. During the winter most ships traveled between Vladivostok, Japan and China.

At the time, many settlements were being founded on the largely uninhabited coastline and it was often necessary to transport entire villages from Vladivostok, including the settlers and all their belongings, supplies and domestic animals. There was a lot of work to do and the ship was always filled with diverse passengers, from various native peoples to the Governor-General. There were Russian officers of all stripes along with their families, farmers with their tools and animals, fishermen, miners, loggers, hunters and gold seekers. By 1918, when I was taking my last trip on this route, 58 villages and various industrial sites had been founded on the coast. When I had first come to the Far East there had been only eight small villages and one logging operation.

3

TOSSED ABOUT IN A TYPHOON

IN NOVEMBER 1909, while en route from Vladivostok to Japan, we survived a large typhoon. When we left Vladivostok, the weather was nice but the next morning all hell broke loose. Early in the morning I could feel in my sleep that the ship had begun to rock increasingly. At 6 a.m. the captain summoned me to the bridge to talk things over. The wind, which had been from the north, had turned to the west and grown into a storm. Because the ship was traveling with no cargo, and was rolling violently with the wind and the waves, we could not keep to our course and our situation was becoming critical as time passed. Accordingly, we decided to turn downwind and, as much as possible, to keep our course toward Japan, hoping to reach the northern coastline and to seek shelter there. Initially the weather was clear but later it began to rain in fits and starts and, as someone from Saaremaa[3] would say,

---

3   Estonia's largest island

to blow hard enough that "a pig would get blown off of its feet".

Heading downwind, it was barely possible to steer the ship. We weren't able to maintain steam pressure because the ship was rolling, and the engine and boiler rooms had taken on a lot of water. Waves crashed relentlessly over the deck and the pumps became clogged. Not much progress was made in pumping any water out, and the ship leaned on its side at about 35 degrees. The next day the storm continued to blow and the water in the boiler room rose so high that two boilers were underwater and their fires had gone out. As the pumps still were not working, we began to bail with the buckets used for dumping boiler ashes overboard. This became very difficult as waves were crashing continuously over the ship, which was rolling heavily. As long as we kept bailing though, the water level didn't get much higher. We smashed the watertight bulkhead between the engine room and the main cargo hold in order to equalize the water level inside the hull. This provided a temporary relief inside the engine room. In the end, there were only two fires still burning. All others were underwater and had gone out, so we were operating at a steam pressure of only 30 pounds instead of the normal 180 pounds of pressure.

The storm raged for five days, gradually fading towards the end and the wind shifted to the north, which was very helpful as it took us closer to the Japanese coast. Otherwise, it was possible we could miss Japan altogether and end up in the Sakhalin narrows where there was no shelter. We always had two men on watch. No one even had time to think about a proper meal and we chewed on whatever raw food came to hand.

Whoever wanted to sleep had to tie himself to something fixed. Once when I was dead tired from the many days of non-stop work, I tried to sleep on the floor of the mess by wrapping some rope around myself and tying the ends to a chair that was fastened to the floor. Getting proper sleep however, was out of the question under the circumstances.

Days and nights passed, seeming immeasurably long, and our limbs were stiff from the cold and damp. In this situation, I saw once again how man can battle against nature with unearthly strength when life is at stake. On the evening of the fifth day, during a snowstorm, we spotted the light of a Japanese lighthouse. At the same time, a large wave crashed over the stern, breaking the steering chain and the ship's wheel, and smashing the second-class cabins. As most of the passengers had taken shelter in the mess, there were no injuries. The rudder, being left to the vagaries of the waves, started thrashing around frightfully and soon disintegrated, its fragments disabling both propellers.

We finally saw land downwind and, with no time to spare, took some soundings and found 14 fathoms of water, so we dropped anchor along with all the chain that we had. Then we waited anxiously to see if the chain would hold or snap. The anchor soon held and the bow began to turn into the wind. The bow was high above the ocean and as most of the water taken on had made its way to the rear of the ship, the stern was barely above water. The bow saved us though, as water beat under the hull and the ship danced like a bottle on the waves without putting too much stress on the anchor.

It was nighttime so we set off some distress flares. However, as powerful waves were thundering onshore, which seemed deserted, no one came. Even if some fisherman had seen us, it was very unlikely that they could safely have reached us. So, we hung on waiting for morning and hoping that the anchor would hold!

With great difficulty, I was able to grasp the thrashing wheel, hang on to it and tie it off. While I was doing so, some people, expecting the chain to break and the ship to be dashed to pieces had, according to Russian custom when facing death, hurriedly put on their finest dry clothes. Clean clothes would also come in handy if it became possible to swim to shore. When I saw what they had been doing, I explained that though it was unlikely that anyone could survive the waves, it was more likely they could do so without any clothes at all because clothing made it easier for the outgoing waves to grab them and pull them back to sea. They promised to shed their clothes at the last moment. The captain, a Latvian, had been on the bridge for the entire storm and now collapsed in a shivering, sodden heap. After the immense stress and strain of the lengthy and powerful storm, he had lost all hope of survival and now wanted to shoot himself.

I comforted him as best as I could, and after a while he settled down a bit and said that he was willing to fight on.

The next morning the wind subsided slightly, raising our spirits, and we started to fix the steering chain. Near the wheel there was a large hole in the deck, through which two men could have squeezed at the same time. Some broken hinge bolts could be seen and what remained of the steering frame and mechanism, while battered, still worked. With tremendous effort, the mechanics were able to pump water from the boiler room, the engine room and the third cargo hold, and so after more than 40 hours dangling at anchor, with the weather now having become quite nice, we weighed anchor and started making our way to the nearest sheltered harbor, at Tsuruga, Japan, about 70 miles to the south. We moved very slowly because one of the propellers had no blades left and the other had only 1½ blades. We made it nevertheless, thanks to the good weather.

We later heard that the storm had been one of the strongest storms in quite some time and had sunk seven Japanese ships near the place we had been. Ships on the Vladivostok route had been marooned in Tsuruga for three days, unable to leave port. It turned out that the Japanese had seen our lights, flags and emergency flares, but as it was impossible to leave shore and come to our aid, they sent a telegram from the lighthouse to the government saying that a ship was in distress. The government had sent a cruiser to help us, which took several hours to reach the location where we had been seen, but by then our ship had disappeared from sight.

In Vladivostok, Count Keyserling and others had not heard from us for seven days and presumed that we had perished at sea. They were very surprised to hear we were in northern Japan, having been on our way to the south.

We stayed in Tsuruga for a week to get things in order and a large tug was sent from Nagasaki to get us. After four days of being towed we at last reached Nagasaki, where we left the ship to be repaired. The captain had approval for traveling to Europe to purchase a new ship, and in his absence I was appointed captain. The second officer, an Estonian by the name of Kärner, became first officer, and the third officer, Siim Roos, also an Estonian, went to Vladivostok onto another ship. He died a few years ago while captain of the *Merisaar*.

4

THE TIME OF THE WORLD WAR

In 1910, after the ship had been overhauled, I went back to Vladivostok and began to sail as captain on many ships for the same firm. In the fall of 1912, I became captain of the *Oleg*, which had recently been purchased from some Norwegians and contracted out to the Chinese. This 2,000-ton ship was the largest in Count Keyserling's fleet. It was a pretty good ship and was the best ocean-going ship I had ever served on. I was *Oleg's* captain until I left Russia in the spring of 1919.

It once happened to me that a recent hire to the crew was an Estonian sailor whose name was well known in Estonian maritime circles. This man was from Kihnu[4] and his name was Umb. In 1887, when he was working as cabin boy on the Estonian ship *Johannes*, he murdered the entire crew, except for the officer, and was sentenced to a forced labor camp on Sakhalin Island. I

4   A small Estonian island

remember my father talking about these horrible murders when I was a little boy, and my recollection remained so fresh that I never would have hired this man. However, the responsibility for hiring the crew belonged to the first officer, and I only heard of the new hire when Umb had already begun working aboard the ship.

My fear of, and distaste for, Umb fortunately turned out to be unfounded. He was a fine and proper man in both his work and his general behavior, and I can even confirm that he was the best man I had in my crew during that time. He had suffered a ten-year sentence of forced labor on Sakhalin and then was required to settle in the Far East. His difficult past had left no visible marks, and in appearance he seemed much younger than his actual age. He was respected by everyone and later left the ship at his own request, hoping to find a better position. I heard nothing about him afterwards.

When the World War began in 1914, I was onboard *Oleg* on my way further north than usual. The ship did not have a radio. After I had left the last port with a telegraph station, the agent had given someone a message to be passed on to me by the last motorboat to leave shore. That person, however, had simply placed the message into the ship's post box and that is where we found it three days later. The message said that, according to the customs agent, Germany had declared war on Russia.

I put some precautionary measures to use, traveling without navigation lights at night and making haste to reach our final destination, where I hoped to receive more details. Reaching there, however, no one knew what was happening, so I explained to them what I'd heard, including to the captain of the fishing fleet's spotting ship, who immediately left for De-Kastri, towards the Amur River, where there was a telegraph station. I picked up a full load of cargo and 300 passengers for the return journey, and made all the usual stops on my route as though everything was normal, except for sailing at night without any navigation lights, just in case. One evening, just before we reached the place that had a telegraph station, the first officer reported seeing two small boats, without navigation lights, heading past us to the north. The boats had seemed Russian. From his report, I surmised that something was happening and as we approached Tetuhe Bay, I saw from a distance that the entire shore was filled with people.

The agent came onboard right away and said the war had been going on for seven days, that the whole world was at war and that I had several piles of telegrams, one from our office in Vladivostok and another from the town of Olga, and that I had to take 2,500 Chinese miners onboard and seven German engineers, who were prisoners. As there was only one police officer in the region, I had to take the prisoners under my protection and also see that they did not escape. There were also Russian passengers, some who had been called to the army and others who had recently lost their jobs because the zinc mines in Tetuhe had closed right away, as most of the capital behind them was German. Altogether, 3,000 people were to be taken onto the ship.

I explained that it would not be possible to take this many people onboard because we had a full load of cargo and were already carrying 300 passengers, both fisherman and other travelers. We also had many large fir logs on the deck. The agent replied that another ship, *Georg*, had received a telegram in Olga with instructions to return to Vladivostok right away, and had left Olga without delay. She had not taken any passengers onboard and had also left behind all the foodstuffs meant for Tetuhe Bay, where people were already hungry. What would happen if another ship didn't come for maybe a few weeks or months? I thought about dumping the logs into the sea because there was no time to take them to shore, but as the ship had already sent out invoices, the entire loss would be borne by the ship owner. Because of this, I decided to leave the logs on board no matter how things were sorted out with all the people. So we started to load and in a few hours everyone was onboard. There were so many people that moving about took great effort and some people suffered and were trod upon, but there were no complaints.

Then, an order came from Vladivostok to rush straight there upon receipt of the telegram, along with instructions on how to undertake this trip, as the order also contained the news that the German cruiser *Emden* was in the Sea of Japan and had already captured the vessel *Rjazani* of the volunteer naval fleet. I was advised to leave everything and everyone there and to proceed directly to Vladivostok without stopping at any port en route. Those from Olga, however, pleading as friends and soldiers, said they had been summoned to help in the war and had no other way to get to Vladivostok and would be court-martialed if I did not help them. Telegrams from government officials threatened to turn me over to the military court if I didn't return with the ship. So please, here you are, what to do!

Tetuhe wanted to know if I was going to Olga or not. I replied that I didn't know yet, that it depended on the situation there, and I asked them to send a telegram to Olga saying just that. I had already decided to go there nonetheless, hoping that things were not so bad. I hadn't told anyone this, though.

It was just beginning to get dark when we left Tetuhe, and fog covered the sea. The distance from Tetuhe to Olga was 57 miles and we arrived in Olga's harbour in the early morning, still in dense fog. I hadn't given the whistle so no one heard us arrive. People were already waiting, however, and shouts of "Hurray, *Oleg* has arrived!" could be heard and spread like wildfire through the town so that soon everyone was running — those going to Vladivostok and those seeing their family members off to war.

I gave everyone two hours to gather onto the ship and then we continued our journey, to my great pleasure still in thick fog. The fog is usually so thick in the region that there could be no question of being tracked by the *Emden*. We traveled in thick fog until evening and then the weather cleared. I immediately kept the ship close to shore where the many small bays would provide good hiding spots if anything should happen. As we did not see anything, and night came, I hurried on with the load of people.

Early the next morning we arrived at Askold Island, with all our lights on, as I had been instructed to do. A motorboat sped up right away and asked which ship we were. When hearing the *Oleg*, we were instructed to drop anchor until daylight, and then to take a specific course from Askold to Vladivostok. We arrived safely in Vladivostok where the harbour was filled with Russian, English and other ships, including a German one that had already been confiscated. The *Oleg* was so overloaded with people that there was no empty space and there were even so many people on the command bridge that I hardly had room to move about, but there was nothing to be done. During our journey, three Chinese had fallen overboard and drowned, which I heard about only after we reached Vladivostok. With such a large load of people it was a blessing that more had not died.

Later, I survived a typhoon aboard *Oleg* in the Pacific Ocean, while taking the empty ship from Nagoya to Nagasaki. An unusually large wave came over the stern, smashing the handrail, the doors and the furniture in the second class cabin, and filling the third class cabin about a third full of water. The hatches were damaged and the wave reached the bridge, yet no people were injured. The force of the wave threw me against the edge of the table and I fell down and was carried to my bunk. After a while the pain subsided and fortunately my ribs were all intact. During the storm a waterspout shot over the ship and landed about 10 fathoms away. I had not seen a waterspout so closely before, nor have I since, but on my travels I had seen quite a few. Still, it's impossible to adequately describe the large roar and the wind when the waterspout went over the ship, which didn't last longer than about half a minute.

In 1915, I was with *Oleg* under contract in Southern China, traveling between Hong Kong and Indochina, carrying sugar, rice, palm oil, teak logs and all that we came across, in smaller or greater quantities. Because it was wartime, French forces were very conscious of their duty and looked diligently at everything involving the ship's crew, fearing spies. During 1915 there were no problems but in 1916 doubts began to arise about us, for some reason. Perhaps the French thought that we were really Germans after all, and things became increasingly complicated. Searches of the ship became more frequent and we were awkwardly watched when we went ashore. This lasted until April without too much inconvenience.

At the beginning of April, we went from Hong Kong to Saigon, where I had already been many times with the *Oleg*. When our ship was met at the river mouth, an official looked at our passports and asked why no one had a photo in their passport. I replied that we were unaware of any law requiring this. We had all been on the crew list since last year, in accordance with Russian law, and the Consul General in Hong Kong had yet to demand this from us. The man shook his head. I saw that something was up, however we were nonetheless allowed to proceed to Saigon.

After we arrived in Saigon and tied up the ship, there was a policeman on the wharf who advised me that not one person was allowed to leave the ship. I waited to see what else would happen. Then the Russian Vice-Consul arrived, a Frenchman, who understood nothing other than the French language and official authority. He asked for permission to search the ship, which I granted. The ship was searched in detail and though nothing was found, the Consul said the ship was under arrest and only I could go ashore. I asked if Russia was at war with France. The answer was no, and that matters would be sorted out the next day. That's as far as things got that day and, because we were under arrest, unloading the ship was out of the question.

The next morning I took M. Veide, the Estonian captain of the SS *Eugenia*, with me to see our agent, who was also the Japanese Consul. I had eight Japanese stokers on board and I asked the Consul that if Russians were not allowed to disembark that was one thing, but why were the Japanese not allowed off the ship? I asked him to accompany Captain Veide and myself to the Russian Consul and then for all of us to visit the Governor together, because while the agent spoke English well the others did not. We proceeded to the Russian Consul where I demanded an explanation for what was happening, and presented Captain Veide from the other Russian ship to him. He (*Veide*) knew each of us personally and would also witness whatever reason was to be given for the arrest of my ship.

There was a lot of heated discussion between the agent and the Consul and it looked like they were going to come to blows. We did not understand what was going on and hoped the agent was acting in our interests. Eventually, we were asked to wait there and the agent and the Consul went to see the Governor. After a while they came back and told me to go back to the ship, as the detainment was to be ended. I asked when unloading could begin and the response was that everything would be resolved the next day, and the morning after that the consul himself would come to the ship.

Back at the ship we saw that the policeman was already gone and we waited to see what the next day would bring.

The Consul arrived before lunch, bringing some of the ship's papers with him, and showed where he had made a notation on the ship's registration that the ship had been requisitioned by the Russian government and had to leave right away and go directly to Vladivostok. I responded that to carry this out the ship required a bunker load of coal and water for the boilers, as well as a stockpile of food. I added that there apparently was a strong NW monsoon brewing and heading out into such a storm with an empty ship was a very big risk. I asked for permission to carry a load of rice and to deliver this to Hong Kong, from where the Consul General would send us on to Vladivostok. The Consul replied that he could not let us have anything and that we had to leave. I then asked permission to send a telegram to the Consul General in Hong Kong, to which he finally agreed, thus delaying the ship's departure by a day.

The Consul returned to the ship at the same time the following morning, said that a reply was apparently not coming, and demanded that I leave. If I didn't comply he would arrest me, put another captain on the ship and send it to Vladivostok. I was a soldier, having been conscripted at the start of the war, but had been sent back to be a ship captain. Now, I thought it would be better to leave and to try escaping to Hong Kong. The Consul General there would surely provide coal and water and we had enough of both to reach Hong Kong. So we left, starting our return trip empty.

Everything went well, but near the Paracel Islands a monsoon with rain became so strong that the ship could no longer be steered with the rudder. We drifted toward the Paracels, which were about 30 miles downwind. After a few hours, the wind turned to the west and this helped us drift towards the north. I was never able to determine how close we had been to the islands because nothing could be seen in the storm and the rain, and the island with the highest elevation was only three feet above sea level. At last, after six days, we reached Hong Kong.

I delivered my report to the Consul General, a Baltic-German by the name of Oetingen, with whom I was familiar because I had been sailing in and out of Hong Kong for about 8 months. After reading my report, he said that he never received my telegram and, if he had, of course he would have allowed the supplies that I had requested, for the reasons noted, and maybe he had received notice from the Russian fleet commander, Admiral Schultz, to requisition the *Oleg* and send her to Vladivostok, but there was no rush with this. I said that all of us aboard the ship were very hurt at being made laughingstocks of in front of the other foreign vessels in Saigon and that I would give a detailed report about this to the Admiral in Vladivostok, with which he agreed.

I then asked him for coal and water, which he initially refused, explaining that he had received no order for this. I explained that the ship had been requisitioned by the Russian government and that the state of Russia was now in control, not the previous ship owner, and that as I did not have any coal and water needed to return to Vladivostok, he had to provide these to me or I would remain standing there while he let Vladivostok know the situation, because I could go nowhere until I received some coal.

I don't know if he ever advised Vladivostok or not, but after lunch both coal and water were brought to the ship and I went to ensure that we were cleared to leave. That evening we departed from Hong Kong. We arrived uneventfully in Vladivostok on the 16th or 17th of April, 1916. A guard boat brought some officials, including a doctor and some military personnel, and the ship was arrested again. They said, however, that this was just going through the motions as the ship now belonged to the government and until everything was settled they were responsible and I was subject to their authority. They promised that things would be resolved by that evening.

We had some French wines on onboard, of course, and everyone was very satisfied after a few glasses, particularly because, at the time, there was already a ban on alcoholic drinks. And so the government took control of the ship that day, the arrest was ended and a list of the ship's crew was requested but could be provided on another day. The next day it seemed that a committee of sorts was created from naval officers and the management of some private shipping firms and the ship was transferred, as it was, to the private shipping company Dobrovolnõi Flot. Along with all the officers and sailors, I stayed on to work for the private shipping firm.

In Vladivostok I reported all that had happened to us in Saigon to Admiral Schultz, including the conditions under which I had been forced to sail from there. Two months went by and I had already forgotten about this event, when one day I was invited to naval headquarters and shown a letter from the Consul and Governor in Saigon, who very much regretted the incident and asked for an apology to be conveyed to me. All is well that ends well, but I have to say that the Russian government officials made mistakes which, as they say in Estonia, would have made even a horse laugh, though no one cared that because of these mistakes my crew and I almost perished on the Paracels.

That summer I began to sail the coast to Pri-Amursk again and in the winter to Japan and China. I brought war materials from Japan to Vladivostok, from where it was trans-shipped to Europe. Life was good and at that time nothing was happening in Vladivostok for us to notice that a world war was raging.

I once had a conflict with the War Governor of Pri-Amursk that could have ended very badly for me, but which ended happily after all. Late one fall, I was sailing toward the Strait of Tartary,[5] almost 700 miles to the north of Vladivostok, to pick up some workers who had been installing a 200-mile long telegraph line through primeval forests from De-Kastri south to Imperatorskaja Gavan. FrThree hundred men were working there in several places and I had let them ashore that spring, where they then began to chop down trees and to do other work. In the summer I had brought them some food supplies and other gear and now this trip was to bring them back, as it was already very late in the fall, snow was on the ground and it was cold. The aforementioned Governor was on board the ship, on his inspection trip. The Governor was paid by the government for each mile traveled on his journey of inspection, but only for travel within the boundaries of his responsibility. This is why he lost all interest in continuing as soon as we had left the area he was responsible for, and he immediately ordered me to take the ship back to Vladivostok so he could return home as soon as possible.

I categorically refused to carry this out, explaining that my orders had not been changed and we were to go to the north and pick up close to 300 people and some horses, who had been informed that I was coming on these dates to pick them up, and who were waiting at a specific place on the coast to avoid losing any time. In addition, I had a notice from the main post office that their food had already run out and I definitely needed to bring these people back. Our office had agreed to this and if we now left them there for another couple of weeks and then returned, what would become of these people? Also, the Strait

---

5   Also called the Strait of Sakhalin

of Tartary was very stormy at this time and there was no shelter nearby. It was only possible to load people in good weather and the Governor should have dealt with the office about this earlier. I could not do otherwise or these people would be without the food and equipment required to spend the winter in that far and hard to reach place, and would perish.

The Governor thundered but could not do anything more as I stuck with my decision. I seriously thought and feared that the Governor could, because it was wartime, create a lot of trouble for me later. The Governor was so angry at my refusal that he did not say a word to me for three days.

When we arrived at the location for picking up the almost 300 telegraph workers, we couldn't do so because of rough seas. They had to travel three miles to the north, through brush and deep snow, to another place where we hoped to be able to take them aboard. When we finally got them all on the ship it was nightfall, and we saw what poor and shabby condition they were in and how hungry they were. They had run out of food three days ago. Seeing this, the Governor forgot his anger at me and acknowledged that I had done the right thing.

Later, arriving in Vladivostok, the Governor was very friendly towards me and left the ship with thanks.

One time during 1917, I had an unusual marine experience with *Oleg*. I arrived at Ohotsk to drop off some supplies for gold miners and fishermen. There was a small harbor at the river mouth that only very small ships could enter. We stopped at sea, at a distance of about 1½ miles from the harbor, needing to unload a cargo of about 1,000 tons of food supplies. For the return trip I was to take some fishermen and their summer's catch to Vladivostok.

At first there were a few days of nice weather and then a storm broke out, putting an end to unloading using boats. It was late fall and there was no more good weather to wait for. Because of this, I went ashore to see if there was any way to take the ship into the harbor, where it would be possible to unload and then load the ship without any disruption. The river mouth was awfully narrow and there was a very strong current. In addition, it was necessary to turn the ship 90° after entering the mouth of the river, and the current made it very difficult to do so.

I decided to risk it nevertheless and, thanks to my significant experience in these waters and my thorough knowledge of the ship, I was fortunate to safely squeeze the ship into the harbor. The ship was secured using the anchor and cables and unloading began again, no longer affected by the storm.

The wind increased in the evening and I dropped a second anchor and also the kedge anchor. In addition, I had a number of cables securely fastened onto some buildings there. A hurricane broke out. The ship stayed in place, barely, thanks to my decision to have the engine running at half throttle to relieve stress on the anchors and the cables so they would not break. The wind howled and roared for what seemed like forever. We lost all contact with land. By morning the hurricane gave way and it became quiet. We went onto the deck to continue working and saw that the river mouth had disappeared. The hurricane had filled the river mouth with sand, so that we were now standing behind a wall of sand that separated us from the sea. It was a hopeless situation.

Nonetheless, we eventually managed to escape and to leave. The natives suggested that we dig a small trench in the sand with shovels, along which water started to flow that, eventually, over one and a half days, washed the river mouth open again.

At the same time the tide rose by about 24 feet and a current began to flow in the river mouth with a speed of 10 knots. I did not dare to keep the ship there any longer and went right out to sea. There was still stormy weather at sea, though, which did not allow any work to go on. I waited there for 1½ months, during which time we were able to work on only one day. It was already getting too late and when ice finally formed in the river mouth, I was forced to leave because we were running out of coal, food and water. I took along 800 Russians and 150 Japanese. We had very little water and I allowed each person only one glass per day.

I initially sailed to Nagasaki, Japan to let the Japanese off the ship. Japan was in the midst of the influenza disease. The first and second officers, and many crewmen, soon became ill in the harbour. The ship had barely left the harbor when I was stricken. I was able to be sick for only 24 hours because then the third officer became ill and I had to go onto the bridge. I wasn't able to remain standing on the bridge, so I gave orders while lying down. Everyone later regained their health and our journey to Vladivostok continued along the usual route.

Sailing along the Far Eastern coast was very stressful and tiring. There were no detailed charts and little was known about ocean depths in the region. Reliance on previous experiences and habits was needed to, as they say, feel and fumble the way around the coast. Most of the places for ships to stop were along the open coast and thus fully exposed to the weather, which made it more difficult to load and unload ships. Further, these waters were subject to thick fog from May through the end of August, and on some journeys, no land could be seen at all. I became familiar with the ship's whistle and its echo against the shore. The echo was unique at each stop and my ear became able to tell different echoes apart until finally I was unerringly able to know where I was.

Because the shipping lines received financial support from the government, ships sailed according to a timetable. The shipping line for which I sailed kept the following schedule: every two weeks I left Vladivostok and sailed for 1,300 miles, sometimes taking on bunker fuel at Sakhalin Island, which added 360 miles, and carried up to 1,500 tons of cargo to drop off at 58 places and, at each stop, I also loaded cargo for the return trip until the holds were full. I needed to sail through each stop because although some places had only one passenger or other goods to come on board, the shipping agreement required that the ship had to stop everywhere or, if there was a complaint, the ship had to pay a cash fine.

Of course, the government always gave the words of a farmer, or almost anyone else, more consideration than the actions taken by the ship or the ship's log. Administering all of this was a tremendous bother but overall things were generally peaceful, and I was given thank you letters from most places during the 10 years that I sailed there as an officer and captain. There was no way to travel in the region other than by sea. A footpath used by hunters went over the mountains, but others used this path only in extreme circumstances.

In the Spring of 1918, in January, I made a report that, due to my health, I could no longer sail on this most challenging route of the shipping line, and I asked to be transferred somewhere else. This was acknowledged. When I arrived back from a trip one time I was requested to go to the office, where I was advised that I could not be transferred because they had no one to replace me.

Arguing didn't help. Due to the war and the new Bolshevik regime, I decided to resign. At the end of March 1919, when I brought the ship to Shanghai for an overhaul, I found myself a new job.

I returned the ship to Russia, and before starting my new job I took a vacation in Japan to treat my rheumatism. From there, I sailed to China.

5

IN CHINA ON THE YANGTZE RIVER

CHINA. THIS country was, and is now, a large and peculiar land of about 400 million people. Though the Chinese still lag far behind Europeans in terms of their civilization and its capabilities, the needs of their large population are enormous. Because the Chinese have not been able to successfully import all of the foreign goods that they need or to successfully sell their locally produced goods to other countries, businessmen of all races and from all of the world's nations have spread to China to help manage China's trade and to get a piece of this land's riches. The world's largest companies all have offices or agents here.

I ended up in the employ of the Standard Oil Company, an American firm and one of the richest companies in the world. Their specialty is petroleum and related products. With US$4.5 million of capital, this firm owned the largest oilfields, oil wells and refineries anywhere in the world. In addition, it owned a large fleet of ships, primarily tankers. The Company brought oil to China's coast with their large ocean-going tankers and then transferred the oil products to the firm's smaller tanker ships for the journey inland. In addition to having large offices in the cities, our Company had representatives throughout China, even in distant inland villages.

After arriving in China, I soon learned that while the Chinese population was very large, all of the most senior and important official positions were in the hands of white men, including the postal service, customs, railway, harbor master, etc.

The same was true with the shipping business. The Chinese held management positions only when operating their rudimentary sailboats, called junks, of which there were an enormous number. All other ships had crews consisting of Chinese sailors, but the management of each ship was in the hands of whites, even on the few steamers that belonged to individual Chinese owners.

Foreign interests, primarily English, Japanese, Norwegian and American owned most of the working ships on China's inland waters. I preferred American ships because they allowed Estonians to sail as captains, while the ships of other nations usually insisted that the captain be of their own nationality.

In May 1919, I began working at Standard Oil Company. For the first month, I was First Officer on the steamer *Mei An.* We carried salt from the mouth of the Yellow River to the Yangtze River. Then I became captain of the motor vessel *Mei-Kiang,* a tanker, on which we sailed from Hankow up to Changsha in Hunan province, and Ichang. Later I began to sail between Nanking and Chinkiang.[6]

From then onwards, I sailed only on the Yangtze River, so let

---

6   Zhenjiang

33

me briefly introduce this large river to you, the reader.

Rivers have a great importance in China because they provide the only major means of transportation. This enormous land has no modern roads or railways. Of China's large rivers, the most important are the Yellow River in the north and the Yangtze River in central China.

As the Yellow River is shallow and unnavigable by large ships, the Yangtze River has immeasurable importance because it goes deep inland and connects China's large interior regions to the ocean and the outside world.

The Yangtze River is about 3,200 miles long. It starts in Tibet and passes through all of southern China before arriving at the East China Sea. The river is the most extensive, important and cheapest transportation link within China, and is navigable for the first 1,550 miles upriver from the river mouth.

The navigable portion of the river is divided into three areas: downriver — from the river mouth to Hankow; mid-river — from Hankow to Ichang; and upriver — from Ichang to Suifu.[7] The downriver length is 620 miles, the mid-river length is 380 miles and the upriver length is 550 miles.

The ability of ships to navigate the river depends on the depth of water. The current can increase significantly at times, depending on the frequency of rainstorms, which can sometimes last for weeks. Water levels increase in the summer due to snow melting in the mountains of Tibet. The increase in water volume is often so large that the river overflows its banks and large areas are flooded.

Floods occurred every year in July and August, even though levees had been built on the river to control floods. The largest flood occurred in 1931, at a scale not seen for 300 years.

---

7   Yibin

At the time, I was captain of the tanker *Mei Foo*. During the flood, we used sandbags to barricade all the gates to the storeroom courtyard, and we pumped floodwater from the yard to protect the buildings and the stores.

There had been heavy rains during July, which raised the water level four feet higher than normal. The heavy rains and the Tibetan snowmelt had brought so much water that the river was unable to guide it all out to sea, and the 600-foot elevation drop from upriver made things even worse. In the mid-river and downriver sections, water ruptured dams and flooded land along the river for 600 miles.

Many people died and much property was lost, however no one knows how many or how much because no statistics were kept. From all of the affected regions, an estimated 6 - 7 million people lost their lives.

The storms and the water also destroyed the levees, and water flowed into the cities. Hankow was up to 10 feet under water and the lower floors of all buildings were flooded. People moved about on the streets using boats. Houses collapsed and trapped people underneath them, as Chinese homes are very flimsily built. Various diseases broke out from the lack of hygiene, the cold and the starvation. People lived in the upper stories of houses and on the railway bed, which was higher, as the railway was no longer running anyway. In some places people lived in water up to a foot deep. Conditions were also poor in the mountains outside of towns, where some people had climbed into trees to escape the water.

The Chinese government, international organizations and especially the Americans helped the Chinese, but many starved to death nonetheless. People were spread out, they were up in trees, they were everywhere. During floods, junks were used to reach and help those who were suffering. Many animals also drowned.

Chinese are fatalists. They prayed and they begged, but there was no panic. They accepted their fate as inevitable — after all, there was flooding almost every year and water broke through dams. The valley was so fertile that if every fifth year was a good year, the yield from such a good year could feed the population for five years.

The Chinese are not a particularly religious people. They honor and pray more to evil spirits than to God. The Chinaman says that God is already a good person but the devil needs to be paid off so he will not cause harm and will leave the Chinaman in peace. They have figurines that they pray to, but seamen do not carry these along with them.

They go to temples to pray to God. Chinese temples are all on high-mountain tops and it almost always takes many hours to get to there. The priests probably thought that this would be good for wealthy, overweight Chinese — good for their health because they have to climb up there alone — without their bearers. Wealthy Chinese go to such places and pray to the Gods once a year.

Spiritual Chinese wear grey and black robes similar to those worn by Catholic priests, and they have pearls around their neck.

When a Chinese person dies they always want to be buried at home — where they were born. If, for example, a Chinaman dies in Hankow but is from somewhere else, his body is placed in a coffin and left on the ground near Hankow. Coffins are always placed side by side and never on top of one another, and are left out in the sun for two years. When a certain number of coffins have accumulated — deceased who have been there for at least two years — a junk is rented and loaded with these coffins and they are taken to the birthplaces of the deceased.

Junks laden with coffins can be seen navigating the river. Every junk will not readily agree to transport coffins, though, and recently there were fewer such junks to be seen.

Coffins could be seen everywhere — on the riverbanks, the boundaries of cities and elsewhere. Coffins that were taken to a deceased's birthplace were again placed on the ground there, and not buried underground, and were then covered by soil such that the deceased remained under a mound of it. Such mounds can be seen over the entire country. The fields between Taku and Tientsin are covered in the mounds of the dead.

A Chinese farmer will place his family's deceased on only his own land and will leave them there for forty days before piling soil on them.

Even now, burial places in Shanghai and Hankow are right in the center of the cities. The wealthy pay rent to the city for the land beneath their burial mounds, but will not sell the property, and no one can force them to tidy up the mounds, not even the city, because the Chinese hold their parents, and the dead, in high respect.

Chinese farmers live in especially poor conditions. Their homes do not have any floors, the walls are made from reeds and clay with a straw roof on top, and that is where they live. The houses are damp and unhealthy and the wind blows through them, and because of this they have a lot of rheumatism and other diseases.

Many poisonous snakes climbed aboard the ship during the flood. They were about 2 to 3 feet long and wrapped themselves around the rails where they slept. Many types of snakes could be seen, principally water snakes. One time a 2½ foot long snake managed to make its way to the bridge. I did not notice it when I entered the bridge, but a sailor eventually spotted it and we were amazed to see it. Chinese were used to snakes, knew how to treat snakebites and did not die from them.

It was particularly hard for us to see how the poor lived in China. They were starving and had no shelter, their children were half-naked and they had to put up with all sorts of weather. Thanks to the floods, the Chinese farmer, similarly poor and much exploited, had now lost even the benefit of being exploited.

During the flood, the wealthy citizens of Hankow were better off than the poor because they moved into the top floors of houses and lived there. The rich man in China has no feelings and no empathy for the poor man. Foreigners will help the Chinese poor, but the rich Chinaman will not help the poor Chinaman and says that doing so will hurt the poor more than help them, because then the poor will become parasites and will never want to work again.

The Chinese have even turned begging into a business. There are organized groups of beggars who are directed and used by wealthy shopkeepers. One wealthy Chinaman keeps lots of beggars, paying them a wage and using them to control the business of begging in the cities. It is his business, so he gets most of the earnings for himself. Some beggars are made to appear injured in order to elicit sympathy. Raw meat is somehow attached to their forearm, appearing to passers by as a wound, while at the same time the beggars moan and cry even though there is nothing wrong with them. Children are another matter, the limbs of small children are deliberately broken and they are given other injuries to their legs and feet, etc.

There are ordinary beggars as well, but as it is mainly a business the "working" beggars each have their own places to work and ordinary beggars are not allowed there. Beggars include women with children and of course most of the children are not their own.

The Chinaman knows his own people and that is why he

doesn't give anything to beggars. It is always the white man who gives money to Chinese beggars. During 30 years I have seen a Chinese person give money to a beggar only once or twice. When I've given money myself, every time I have done so I've been told that giving money isn't good and only encourages the business of begging.

The government doesn't bother itself with this kind of business because the policemen benefit from it. The businesses pay them bribes and so they do nothing to prevent the begging. City councilmen cannot afford to lose the begging businesses because China has too many beggars. Foreign papers write about this and how this type of business should not be allowed, but to no effect.

The Chinese are great scoundrels, keen gamblers and large risk takers, and will place their last cent into a game. They do not believe that cheating someone out of something will bring them dishonor, and if they are able to swindle someone they are proud of it.

They play cards and mahjong etc to make money. Even little boys play heads or tails in the streets; a thirst for money is in their blood from childhood.

Chinese have bribery in their blood. Even on our ships it was common to see that when a new member joined the Chinese crew a deal had been made with the Chinaman in charge, the one who earned the most, either the boatswain or a Chinese mechanic, and the bribe taken for giving the position was regularly cashed in when he gave the crew their pay.

Once I wanted to eliminate the practice of bribery aboard my ship, but it didn't work. To try and achieve this goal, I did not give the boatswain money to pay the wages and I paid the Chinese crew myself. The boatswain lost all of his authority and respect with the crew, they no longer obeyed his orders to do work around the ship, and I was forced to dismiss him. The new boatswain, however, continued the custom of taking bribes, which was easier, as he was used to the captain giving the crew's wages to the boatswain, who would then pay the men and also see that they were fed.

Accordingly, boatswain jobs were very lucrative and highly desirable. There were instances where someone who wanted a boatswain's position paid the captain a bribe of up to $1,000.

Occasionally it was necessary to fine the Chinese seamen in some amount. This happened especially often with the helmsmen when they fell asleep at the wheel. In such a circumstance, permission had to be received from the office before a fine could be issued and the amount of the fine had to be sent to the office after it was collected. This was very cumbersome. On top of this, not a single Chinaman believed that the fine would really be sent to the office. They steadfastly believed that the captain would keep the money in his own pocket.

Later on, the captains created their own custom for monetary fines. On payday they ordered the offending man and the boatswain onto the deck and had the boatswain count the fine out in silver dollars so everyone could see. The captain then threw the fine overboard in full view of everyone. By doing so, the man who was fined saw that no one took his money into their own pocket, and thinking that this was an awful waste of money the man tried to improve his behavior.

During the summers' high water levels, ships of up to 18,000-tons can reach Hankow from the sea. Ships of up to 13,000-tons can go 130 miles further inland, to the mouth of the Xiang River, and ships of up to 3,000-tons can go as far as Ichang. To go any further is possible only with special river ships of up to 1,000-tons.

The width of the river varies greatly. Sometimes it is so wide that one can hardly see the banks, and sometimes it is so narrow that ships are unable to pass one another. Submerged rocks and shifting underwater sands present a hazard to ships and impede travel on the river.

During the summer, the current usually averages a speed of 5-6 knots and increases to 20 knots in some rapids. In winter the larger ships are only able to go as far as Wuhu, where the water is up to 20 feet deep.

Navigation during the winter depends on how deep the water is. Normally, large ships can sail to Wuhu. From there it is possible for smaller ships with a draft of up to 12 feet to reach Hankow, or to go even further if their draft is less than that. Going past Hankow is possible only with ships whose draft is less than 6 feet.

Large ships remain moored in the winter and are able to travel in the summer depending on the degree to which the river has been able to clear its bed.

The water brings down enormous quantities of sand from the mountains, making the river water thick and yellow. The sand eventually settles on the riverbed and forms sandy shoals, which do not remain in the same place but move from one place to another depending on the speed and direction of the current. Frequently, a place just sailed through the day before yesterday is an impassable sand bar today. There are about 60 million people living on the Yangtze River and its banks. On average, 3,000 people drown in the river each year. Sailing on the river, I constantly saw bodies of drowning victims being carried downstream by the current.

After a while, I became familiar with how to deal with the Chinese. The sailings were not especially difficult and I had to trust the Chinese pilots completely because I was not familiar with the local conditions.

All Chinese smoke opium, some more, some less, some only during holidays, but there probably is not a Chinese who doesn't smoke opium at all. Opium dens are everywhere. White people also smoke, but not in public. They either go to the opium houses or smoke at home.

On the ship, I could often see the Chinese pilot lying on a mat and smoking an opium pipe. One time the anchor wasn't holding and I called for the pilot to help, but because of the opium he was in such poor shape that he could not do anything — he was dopey, covered in sweat and shaking.

The seamen generally do not smoke opium. They are a healthier group because they earn their living on foreign ships and would not be able to keep their jobs if they smoked. Smoking opium was allowed on the Chinese ships, though, but not aboard foreign ships.

Opium is expensive. A poor man can buy the cheapest kind a few times a month. The Hague Opium Conference did not ban opium but made it costly.

The monopoly over opium is in the hands of generals and governors. They receive the income, and the workers who cultivate the opium do not earn very much.

Chang Kai-shek tried to ban the Chinese people from smoking opium. He issued an order that those who were found with opium would be executed, and searches were organized. He also opened government opium clinics where smokers were treated for the addiction. If someone who had received treatment was caught smoking opium a second time though, they were then executed. The army organized the executions.

As China is generally without any organization whatsoever, it was difficult to control the smoking and so it continued. One time I heard that five people — two women and three men — were executed at once because of opium.

Szechwan Province, 1,390 miles from the mouth of the Yangtze River, is where most of the opium is cultivated. The generals forced people to grow opium instead of rice, and the people remained poor while the generals prospered. Opium was transported downriver by the shipload. Even though this was a very fertile province, the people had nothing but starvation to show for it.

In the Yangtze River region it was already hot in May, although the hottest months were July, August and September. The weather there is similar to that of tropical lands, with large, sudden storms — the typhoons. Being on the river during these storms isn't that bad, as there are places to take shelter. My travel region along the river was within 1,000 miles of the river mouth — the Lower River and the Middle River.

The Yangtze River valley is very fertile and fruit grows there year round. The Chinese achieve three harvests per year without using fertilizer, because the river floods the surrounding land carrying mud and nutrients.

The Chinaman farms in a very primitive fashion, either tilling the soil by hand with a pickaxe or by using oxen. Wagons are not seen in China at all — there are only carts with two wheels that are pulled by oxen. The carts have large wheels, about 3-4 feet in diameter, and are made of wood. When they are moving they make a large clatter. There are also no proper roads in China. Everything is carried on the backs of horses or donkeys, or is carried by people on foot. It is common to see donkeys carrying bags on their backs, however most goods are carried by people using bamboo yokes. All sorts of goods are carried like this, such as rice, and when doing so there are always many Chinese walking together.

The Chinese are pretty good sailors, especially those from Northern China, and they mainly sail on junks. These are cumbersome vessels and only the Chinese have the patience to travel on them.

A 150-ton junk carries 50 men as there is a lot of work to do, and they also need to protect themselves from pirates. Junks always travel together, in groups of up to 200.

The crews on junks are honest seamen and never engage in piracy. Pirates are found everywhere, though, living on land or sailing their junks on the sea.

That fall, after 4½ months, I went back on the *Mei An*, a cargo ship, where I remained captain for 4½ years. During the five months before I became her captain, this ship had six other captains, of every nationality, as she was especially difficult to control.

In June 1924, I returned to my homeland of Estonia for a vacation. The vacation lasted for six months. The return trip home was free and I continued to get paid, but the travel time both ways took three months and so only three months was left for my vacation. This was my first time back home since 1907. I sailed home via America because the route was better and it was not as hot as going via the Suez Canal, which is an uncomfortable trip during the summer.

A lot had changed in my homeland. I felt like it was my land, my inheritance, like it had not been meant for all the Estonian people but was my personal land.

All of my acquaintances seemed to have moved away, some had died, the young ones had grown up and when I arrived on my home island many even seemed to be afraid of me. Most of the time I lived in Kuressaare, the capital of Saaremaa.

My health had suffered in China's climate and I fell ill with an intestinal ailment in my homeland. I went to various doctors and to the hospital, where I was examined by specialists, but no one was able to help me. My health was so poor that I cut my vacation short and left my homeland to die, because if I died while at work, my family would receive a pension.

After I returned from my homeland to China in the fall of 1924, I was given the task of learning how to sail upriver on the Yangtze, This 350-mile long section of the river was especially hazardous and difficult for ships to navigate because of the rapids, where the currents were very strong, even though each rapid was not very long. Only special ships were able to travel upriver. To get to know the upriver section we were required to sail there for three months.

It was especially difficult to navigate the rapids in low water. The ship's engine wasn't powerful enough to take the ship through the rapids and it needed to be heaved through. Ships need to be heaved ahead about a ship length, sometimes more. Only ships that were able to travel at a speed of 17-18 knots were able to make it through the rapids.

The river is very narrow. Several cables are taken up to 800 meters ahead and are fixed to rocks on the bank and then the heaving begins. The engines are running at full throttle. In addition, young bamboo shoots are used to make ropes, which are very strong when they are new. These ropes are used if all the cables break.

Less powerful ships are moved over the rapids with the help of human labor. There are usually up to 1,000 men on the riverbank to help heave ships. Sometimes, when the current flowing through the rapids is very strong, it takes four hours to move a vessel ahead by one ship length.

Many accidents happen during the heaving, especially if a cable breaks. There are, however, a lot of rapids. Within the same general area, the location of the rapids and the speed of the current are always changing, even at the same water level. To help ships on the river, the rocky banks are marked in feet so the depth of water can be seen and taken into consideration for navigating the rapids. The speed of the current can be found in a ledger kept at the site of each rapid. Sometimes a boat needs to be heaved through up to five rapids per day.

Once, when I was learning on the Upper River, I saw a captain who, after heaving his boat several times in one day, was unable to write in the evening because his hand shook so much from the stress and fatigue. Due to the hazards of the Upper River, 1/3 of the ships that travel there are lost in the average year and another third are damaged.

I sailed on the Upper River for 14 years, summers and winters, and only rarely sailed on the lower portion of the river. The ships that traveled on the Upper River during the winter were small, only 100 to 150-tons, and they were able to travel only if the water was at least six feet deep. The ships could not be longer than 140 feet because the river was narrow. Traveling during the winter was especially dangerous.

There are lucky and unlucky ships. One English boat had an accident every other trip and was constantly being repaired. This boat had various captains and pilots and eyes were drawn on it because Chinese boats on the river all had eyes painted on them. A Chinese priest was even brought to bless the boat and to give it a new name, but nothing helped. A mistake of some kind had obviously been made during the boat's construction, because nothing helped it to avoid accidents.

When I began to sail on the Upper River I was the officer on the tanker *Mei Chuen*, a steamship. I was on her, to learn, for twelve trips.

As a seaman, I understood that by being observant and paying careful attention to commands, it was possible to travel even on this river. Our captain had sailed there for seven years, but he took too many risks and it finally caught up with him. It was a difficult trip on July 12, 1924. There were shadows between the mountains and there was no visibility, and the pilot did not want to take us any further but the captain nevertheless insisted that he do so, and thus we ran aground on some rocks. I heard a crushing sound below but I couldn't see anything, so I ran down to see what had happened. The first room, the engine room, was half filled with water and I yelled upstairs that we were sinking. The mechanic said that there was no escape other than we had to pump out the oil, and he started to do so without asking the captain for permission. The captain turned the ship around and took us straight toward the bank. I ordered the Chinese crew to go below to the other deck and to close all the windows and doors, but they were too afraid to obey. So I went myself, even though I was swimming in oil.

The ship's stern rose as the oil was pumped out and soon the bow was on the riverbank. The ship was already almost on its side but I managed to get out and not get caught underneath. We carried the anchors onto land so the ship would not slide back into the deeper water.

A few hours after swimming in the oil, I began to experience pains. It felt like my skin was being pricked with needles. I had a fever — I had burned all of my skin in the oil, except for on my face, and my skin peeled off.

After a while, an American warship came to protect us from bandits. This ship had a doctor on board and he smeared a salve on my skin and then bandaged me up. I was in bed for two days.

It took a month to repair the ship. Cement was used to fill all of the cracks. Half of the ship's hull had come off — to the second boiler room. It took 120 drums of cement to finish the repairs. After that we went to Shanghai for an overhaul.

With this, my learning period ended. In the spring, I became captain of *Mei Tan*, an upriver tugboat. It was nasty sailing there.

The big ships created large waves in the middle of the river and swamped each passing tug, so every place on board was wet. This ship was able to travel at 17 knots per hour.

Mine was the first boat to leave in the mornings and the last to return to anchor in the evenings, by which time the other faster ships had taken all of the best places to drop anchor and I was unable to find a favorable place for my ship. It was a very difficult job, but I knew two captains who had worked here before and I believed that whatever they had put up with, I could manage as well.

6

THE BRITISH CONFLICT WITH YANG SEN

DURING 1926, I was upriver with *Mei Tan* in my first year as her captain, when a conflict began between the British and General Yang Sen from the city of Wanhsien. Wanhsien was one of the largest producers of wood oil and about 150,000 tons per year of this expensive oil was exported, at 400-600 Chinese dollars per ton, to Europe and even more to America, for use in high quality oil paints and lacquers. Over the years, my ships carried 30,000 tons of this oil down from Wanhsien and Chungking.

Wanliu, a passenger steamer owned by Butterfield & Swire, a British firm, left Ichang going towards Chungking a few days before I did. The next day some soldiers loyal to Yang Sen wanted to get aboard and sail to Wanhsien. The British government had strongly forbidden the transport of Chinese soldiers on private ships, and other countries had also forbidden this, because the generals were fighting against one another and if a ship were carrying another general's soldiers it would be shot at more than usual.

In this case, the captain, seeing some soldiers approaching his ship by boat, gave the order to depart and sailed away leaving the soldiers behind. The ship passed by Wanhsien on the same day, where it briefly stopped, and then proceeded towards Chungking. The ship *Wantung*, belonging to the same company, was heading downstream and arrived in the evening at the same town of Wanhsien. Yang Sen took his soldiers aboard and seized the ship. Similarly, *Wanhsien* was seized the next day when she arrived from Ichang.

The British gunboat *Cockchafer* was in Wanhsien and had two 6-inch guns and other arms, but her captain thought it best not to immediately turn this into a clash but to attempt to resolve the situation through discussion, as was done every day. The Chinese soldiers, however, numbering close to 300 on each ship, were behaving very defiantly towards the captain and officers of one of the ships, who were left with no choice but to barricade themselves behind the steel shutters on the bridge, after having the foresight to gather some food, so they wouldn't fall into the hands of the soldiers.

General Yang Sen complained that the boats carrying the soldiers left behind by *Wanliu* had been swamped and submerged by the wake from *Wanliu* pulling away, that these soldiers had all drowned and that 75,000 Chinese silver dollars aboard the boat had been lost. He demanded compensation for the souls of the dead soldiers and the return of the lost money from the shipping company, otherwise the ships would not be returned. In the meantime, 20,000 of Yang Sen's soldiers had settled in on both banks of the river in case *Cockchafer* tried to do anything to free the ships. Britain had no consul in Wanhsien, so the consul from Chungking had to come on another British warship to try and settle things, even as it was certain that this was another of Yang Sen's fabrications. While the soldiers actually could have drowned, there certainly had been no money there. Further, the captain and crew of *Wanliu* confirmed that no boats had capsized and the captain of an American ship that had been sailing to the rear had not seen anything, such as a piece of a boat or anything else, which should have been there if the story had been true.

A few days later, going past Wanhsien on my way to Chungking, I saw two British ships at anchor close to town near *Cockchafer*. I passed by them fairly closely. I saw many Chinese soldiers on board but not a single member of the ship's crew, who were all Europeans, and all the steel shutters around the bridge were closed.

I immediately thought that something must have happened. I saw that both riverbanks were filled with soldiers and I tried to hurry past as I wasn't scheduled to stop here this time.

The next morning, further upriver, I saw a British gunboat stuck bow first in the riverbank. I went to ask what had happened and if help was needed. The response was that they had run aground on a rock because their steering was broken, and they had a leak, but that they would be able to repair it on their own. They thanked us for stopping and we continued on our way.

When we reached Chungking our manager advised me that the situation had become critical. All Chinese employees had left the British ships and had also left *Wanliu*, and *Wanliu's* captain, along with the British consul, had gone to Wanhsien on a warship. That is what I had seen en route. I wasn't going to leave until the dispute was settled and, as my ship would be completely unloaded that day, he asked me to come the next day, Sunday, to visit him at his home in the mountains and to stay with him until Monday morning. Then we would go and visit the captain of the American gunboat to hear how things were developing.

And so on Sunday morning I went up the mountain carried on a sedan chair by four Chinamen, as can be seen in China.

On Monday morning, we went to the American gunboat USS *Palos* and heard that a senior officer and 50 sailors from a British cruiser in Hankow, with the intent of camouflage, had sailed to Wanhsien aboard *Kia-Woo*, a ship that had been painted grey, and had immediately gone alongside *Wanhsien*.

The Chinese did not recognize the ship, accepted the ropes offered and secured them to their own ship. Then, the British jumped over the rails wanting to rescue the captain, the officers and the mechanics, by force if necessary. A brawl started on the ship between the British and the Chinese and the Chinese on land began to attack the British using cannons and guns. *Cockchafer*, and the other gunboat that had come from Chungking, returned fire and it turned into a proper battle.

I was ordered to go to my ship and to fire up both boilers, to load enough food to last for a few weeks and to be ready to leave the stores in 15 minutes to go alongside *Palos*, just in case some trouble were to break loose here. All the Europeans and Americans there came aboard my ship and then I went ahead and *Palos* came behind me, as it was feared that the pilots and crew would abandon the *Mei Tan*. If this were to happen, the gunboat had promised to provide me with a crew but no one was an experienced pilot. Even I, in my first year as a captain here, didn't have much experience, though with a high water level I hoped that I would be able to take the ships down river.

The British crews had left their ships and a French ship had left a day earlier, so no ships were coming upriver any more but were waiting for a solution. Thus, I waited in Chungking for 13 days until things cleared up enough for me to go back downriver, and *Mei Hsia* came in my place as a larger and more spacious ship. Still, things were uneventful in Chungking.

I later heard that when fighting had begun on the deck, the captain and officers of *Wanhsien* had charged out from the bridge and climbed onto the roof of the *Kia-Woo's* bridge, which was alongside, and from there had managed, uninjured, to get onto the bridge itself. The Chinese all ran below deck to find shelter in the engine room and wherever else they could, leaving the dead on the deck, including the British commander and three British sailors. *Kia-Woo* then cut loose from *Wanhsien* and pulled in behind *Wantung*, where they saw her captain strung out on the stern by a rope. He was cut down and saved, as were the second officer and a mechanic, who ran along the deck and jumped onto the *Kia-Woo's* prow, as she had been keeping herself nose first in *Wantung's* stern. The first officer jumped overboard and swam to the French gunboat that wasn't very far away. The other mechanic, an older man, also charged into the water but he drowned.

While all of this was going on, the two British gunboats and *Kia-Woo* kept both *Wanhsien* and *Wantung* under constant machine gun fire so the Chinese soldiers could not come back onto the deck and interfere. From the riverbanks, however, the 20,000 Chinese soldiers fired at the gunboats with cannons and other firearms, though their aim was poor and most shells flew by, except for one that smashed the motorboat hanging at the rear of the French gunboat. Almost all of the men on the decks of the gunboats were wounded but fortunately there were no deaths.

The British then went downriver from Wanhsien continuously firing their guns and caused heavy casualties for the Chinese, who had arranged their cannon batteries so poorly along the riverbank that they could easily be seen, and when British shells hit one, which happened every time they took a shot, the battery was completely destroyed. Both soldiers and civilians came down to the river to watch what was going on, thinking that the British would not dare to engage such a large army. There were also stories circulating that the British 6-inch guns were made of wood and couldn't fire a single shot. Now, however, they became personally familiar with these wooden cannons. Thousands of Chinese were killed, and for two years afterwards British ships were not allowed to stop there. British casualties, as I mentioned above, were one officer and 3 sailors. The Chinese later released their bodies and they were buried in Ichang.

As by then it was nightfall, the British gunboats dropped anchor about 10 miles below the city and planned to test the Chinese defenses again the next morning. However, they had too many casualties and not enough able-bodied soldiers left, so the next morning they sailed to Ichang.

When I returned to Wanhsien again after 16 days, the two ships *Wanhsien* and *Wantung* were anchored 1–1½ miles below the city. I sailed by them quite closely again. The main cabins of the ships, and everything else, had many bullet holes and what looked like damage from shells, and many of the holes were large enough for people to walk through. A few months later, the ships were returned to their owner and were taken to Shanghai for reconstruction, principally their upper sections.

Yang Sen had previously been very popular among the Chinese, but from then onwards his popularity declined because he had invited this large conflict. Many city dwellers had been killed or wounded and many homes had been reduced to rubble, and there was no hope that any restitution would be forthcoming. Another general later pushed him out of there and he then became a very quiet and poor general somewhere inland, which brought joy to all mariners, because the most undisciplined soldiers in the world were General Yang Sen's. They were not soldiers but were bandits, and had fights or battles with every ship. He sponsored these bandits for the entire 350-mile length of this section of the river, and sometimes even further. Nonetheless, he carried out many improvements to the city of Wanhsien, such as making the streets wider, requiring the Chinese to build multi-storey European style homes, and other modernizations. However, he was on a continuous war footing with others and was a nuisance to everyone, and of course he demanded high taxes from the councilmen of Wanhsien.

Here is a report from Time magazine on the incident, published on September 20, 1926:

Britain Baited
The city of Wanhsien, some 1,200 miles up the Yangtze river from Shanghai, became suddenly last week of world importance as Chinese mercenaries battled there with two tiny British river warships.

One General Yang Sen, a little sloe-eyed commander, 45, nominally subordinate to Super-Tuchun Wu Pei-fu, caused the affray by seizing the British river freight boats *Wan-tung* and *Wanhsien*. General Yang alleged that the *Wanliu*, another British freighter owned by the same company as those seized had previously upset two sampans filled with his soldiers. Despite the protests of the local British consul General Yang placed 300 soldiers on the captured freighters who promptly locked the white officers and passengers in their cabins, fed them but sparingly.

Meanwhile the British auxiliary warship *Kiawo*, a mere, armored river steamer, lay beside the captured vessels, covered at point blank range by the Yang artillery. To break this deadlock, intolerable to British amour propre, H. M. S. *Cockchafer* and H. M. S. *Wigdeon*, both river warships of the highest armament, steamed close to shore, drew the fire of the land batteries and shelled the city of Wanhsien.

The British auxiliary *Kiawo* at once opened fire on the land batteries, and all three British warships steamed close to the captured British merchantmen, in an effort to rescue their officers and passengers. The *Kiawo* steamed under the lea of the Wanhsien and effected a rescue of all Occidentals on board after a hand to hand fight with the Chinese. General Yang's well directed artillery fire made it impossible to board the *Wantung*, but the British warships stood by at a distance and picked up the *Wantung's* crew and passengers who leaped overboard and all swam to safety despite the pot-shotting of Chinese riflemen. The British ships then withdrew out of range of the shore artillery and bombarded Wanhsien, a city of 150,000 population, until fires broke out in every quarter and completed the destruction. Three British officers and four British seamen were killed.

At once Vice-Admiral Sir Edwyn Alexander-Sinclair, commander-in-chief of the British China Station, began to steam portentously up the Yangtze on his flagship, the cruiser *Hawkins*. Sir Edwyn well knew that the potent *Hawkins* could not navigate the Yangtze above Hankow, some 300 miles below Wanhsien, on account of the shallow rapids, most famed of which is the so-called "Tiger's Tooth." But Hankow could be used as a base for punitive expeditions, and a glimpse of the *Hawkins* might strike salutary terror into many a Chinese breast.

7

IN THE VORTEX OF THE CHINESE CIVIL WAR AND REVOLUTION

In 1926, while I was still upriver working aboard the tug, the revolution began. Chiang Kai-shek started attacking to the north from Canton. There was confusion throughout China. Chiang Kai-shek pushed forcefully ahead. The central government fought back, of course, but one general after the other was either defeated or, along with their soldiers, joined forces with Chiang Kai-shek. Some soldiers even became bandits.

China had not actually had a central government since 1911. Each province had its own laws and its own generals, who were in control, and who demanded taxes. Farmers prepaid taxes for 54 years. No general law was in effect.

In the countryside, however, there was continuous general warfare. Battles erupted in five areas where generals were fighting each other.

The population was sympathetic to Chiang Kai-shek, particularly in the south. He wanted a united China and because of this he agreed to receive help from the Russians, who provided him with war materials and other assistance. In the beginning, it seemed to be the start of communism. Strikes erupted everywhere, even on the ship. All Europeans in Hankow went on board ships and warships and lived there. We were required to provide oil to the warships. There were no sailors — I had captains and first officers as sailors. An American warship gave us food. Warships came to Hankow in 1926 and this was the most confusing time. The situation improved in 1928.

While I was staying in Hankow, there were no battles but there was general confusion. No one knew what was going to happen. All sorts of terrible things could be expected. The Chinese became impudent toward white people. Europeans were unable to live in Hankow any longer and were sent to Shanghai. My wife had recently arrived from Europe to join me and she had to wait for 4½ months in Shanghai before we met. It was in 1927, after the strike by Chinese workers in Hankow had ended, and the men had begun to work again, that I received an order to go to Shanghai for an overhaul. I had been longing to escape to there for four and a half months.

All ships working on the Upper River underwent a complete overhaul each year before heading upriver, to ensure they were in good working order for that dangerous section of the river. My ship was overhauled in three weeks and I remained waiting in Shanghai, because the political situation had become quite complex and no one knew what lay ahead.

Chiang Kai-shek's armies from Canton were already near Shanghai, and also near Nanking, however the northern armies and the armies of the previous central government, along with White Russian soldiers, fought back. It was certain, however, that this resistance would not last long because the Chinese were ineffective fighters, there were too few White Russians, and communications between Shanghai and Nanking were already broken.

The sound of cannon fire could already be heard and as the communists surrounded Shanghai on land it was certain that they wanted to conquer the city. Accordingly, all Americans and Europeans were called to serve in the army, along with the small number of soldiers from other nations that were staying there, and were sent to the boundary of the city to protect it. Every country with citizens living in Shanghai's International Settlement has their own trained military unit, fully equipped and supplied by the city of Shanghai. These units are under the ultimate command of the Colonel of the British army. Many of the foreigners living and working in Shanghai have been trained as soldiers and are commanded by officers who, for the most part, have been through the World War, and as things get worse they are called to service on a few hours' notice, each to their own unit. Thus, in a very short time, men can be ready to face every crisis. They are very well equipped and trained and can provide strong resistance to every opponent. The French Concession is protected only by the French army, by themselves, and is comprised of French, Russian and other civilians, similar to how the army is organized in the International Settlement. During times of war and other crises though, they usually worked together.

At this time, however, all countries had relatively few soldiers or warships there so everyone was mobilized and sent, along with sailors from the warships and other units, to the boundary between China and the International Settlement, to push back the communists in case they started to invade. Fast steamships and warships from every corner of the world were hurrying to Shanghai. In the beginning though, there were only a small number of defenders compared to the number of communists. The warships, however, had left just enough of their crew aboard so they could shell the communists across the city.

I lived on Haskell Road near the boundary with the Chinese city of Chapei. The last night that we stayed there before the crisis, I heard explosions all night long at the railway station near us, which was situated on Range Road. Approximately 2,600 White Russians had barricaded themselves in the station and were returning the communists' fire from armored trains. The shells of the communists exploded in the station. It was not possible to even think of getting any sleep because the explosions were so close that as soon as your eyes fell shut, the sound of the next shell exploding had them wide open again. When my wife asked who was fighting all night long, I said that it was the Chinese, in great joy, because they were sympathetic with the communists in Canton, and were letting off rockets or Chinese fireworks, which they do at every opportunity.

In the morning, though, gunshots could already be heard, and quite close to us. I went to my office to get instructions. As I approached the intersection of Haskell and Range Roads, I saw British soldiers using sandbags and barbed wire to barricade the end of Haskell Road where it reached Range Road. There were no instructions for me at the office other than an order to be ready to go, just in case, as the situation was becoming more complicated.

I went back home, where I found Siim Roos, another Estonian captain, who had come from the French Concession to see how we were doing.

We discussed the circumstances and decided to give him some valuables to take to his home for safekeeping. We carried a suitcase out between us to find a car, which we found quite quickly, and Captain Roos went home.

PETER MENDER

When I arrived back inside, I found a letter in the lobby from my office that had been delivered in the meantime. This instructed me to fire up the boilers of my ship, to take a load of bunker oil and to sail out tomorrow afternoon when I was ready. The destination would be provided then. We thought that our daughter should be taken to stay with Captain Roos' family in the French Concession, and that this should be done as soon as she came home from school. I took my daughter there by taxi. While I was gone, the crisis already started because the police had come to each house ordering everyone to evacuate without delay. The White Russians had run out of ammunition and had already retreated across the boundary into the city and now, as the Chinese had a clear road with no opposition, the Chinese communists were expected to reach here by 4 p.m. The armies protecting the city would not start shooting until fired upon by the Chinese, but then it would be too late to evacuate. It was possible that the city's defenses would be overrun and, in that case, all Europeans were to gather on the grounds of the International Settlement behind Soochow Creek. At the time, my wife and I, and the wives of two Latvian seamen, one of whom had a son, were living in the same house.

I went to find a taxi with which to try and save some useful things because, although the communist soldiers might not break through into the city, the house would still be picked clean by Chinese thieves, even under the eyes of British soldiers watching from the front of the house. From the back of the house, however, anyone could force their way in. I wasn't able to find a taxi right away and I had to wait. At last I got one, and then another, which was going to fill up with gas and then follow us. We turned onto North Szechuen Road and went to what used to be the corner of Haining Road, where the driver did not go any further because the street was empty and shooting had begun.

61

He said that he would wait for me there. I then went along the deserted street as bullets struck the walls of homes here and there. I pressed on and soon arrived at the intersection of Range Road and North Szechuen Road, where British and Indian soldiers were exchanging fire with the approaching communists along North Szechuen Road, while themselves lying behind sandbags along Range Road. The soldiers however, did not want to let me through because it was too dangerous. I explained to them that my wife was waiting in the next house. At last, they let me pass and I arrived home. Everyone there had been afraid for my safety, and now it was also necessary to leave right away. I didn't tell anyone that things were quite bad at the intersection of Range Road and North Szechuen Road, as I was afraid they might lose their courage.

And so the five of us began our trip through the hail of bullets. The soldiers let us pass through the barricade again, and told us to be careful as some of the Hindu soldiers had already been wounded and gunfire was also expected from along Range Road. We had to hurry to get away from there, and did so as fast as we could. We heard gunfire from the intersection of Range and North Szechuen Roads as we ran along North Szechuen Road. Bullets flew around us but no one was hit. My wife said that she could not go on, so I threw down the suitcases and grabbed her and dragged her into Haining Road where it was quieter. I then returned for the suitcases, which I was fortunately able to retrieve. I put my wife, along with the Latvian lady and her son, into the waiting taxi, and the other lady into a rickshaw, and said my goodbyes to them and ordered their drivers to go to Capt. Roos' home in the French Concession. Myself, I took a rickshaw and rode over the toll bridge to where our ferrying steamer was moored, which was used to travel to our supply depot, and got a ride to my ship.

Most of my crew was still ashore helping their families. I sent someone to find them with an order to let me know when one of the mechanics had returned. Toward morning, the Second Mechanic, a Chinaman, came aboard and I ordered him to make sure the boilers were lit by first light, and then the rest of the crew began to arrive, one by one, so that most of them were there by daybreak. We now began to weigh the anchors as the ship had been secured, fore and aft, with four anchors. After heaving all of the anchors we went to the bridge to wait for *Mei Hsia* to finish loading bunker oil and then it would be our turn. In the meantime, it was necessary to fuel the American destroyer that had arrived in Shanghai and because of this we weren't ready at the right time. *Mei Hsia* was ordered to depart early in the morning and then I, after loading up with bunker oil. There was nothing for me to do on the ship that evening because destroyers were being refueled all night, so I equipped myself with a couple of revolvers and went ashore to see how my family was doing. Arriving at Capt. Roos' home I found many visitors, as all those living in the Hankow part of town had run away from there — Latvians, Russians, etc. Many of them were seaman we previously knew in Vladivostok, so it was understandable that all those who came were welcomed. I spent the night there and early the next morning I took a taxi from the French Concession to our supply depot, about 7-8 miles distant. I was stopped by patrols several times but when they saw a European and Standard Oil man, I was let through right away.

When I arrived at the ship the bunkering began immediately and we were ready by 10 a.m. I received an order to first go to Nanking, where I would receive another order. So, I left. We had been traveling for over four hours when I saw *Mei Hsia* coming toward us. We both stopped and I heard from her captain that he had gone as far as Vine Point station, about sixty miles from

Shanghai, where he had come under acute gunfire and, not wanting to risk going ahead, he decided to return to Shanghai. I thought that as my ship was much less protected against bullets than his new vessel, and as he was the oldest captain with much experience, I should not have to risk my ship either and so I also turned my ship around and sailed back.

After arriving in Shanghai that evening we were ordered to wait until morning, when an American warship was to take us back upriver in a convoy. I could not go home any more that evening and the next morning we waited for the ships to form the convoy. At last, at 10 in the morning, the captain of *Mei Hsia* and myself were called to the riverbank nearest the town site to talk things over with our manager. When we arrived, the manager advised that despite all of his efforts, he had been unable to arrange for a convoy because the situation here was very critical and all of the ships' crews had been taken ashore to help protect the city. Up until then, the only shooting between the communists and the city's defenders had been on the other bank, and although the Chinese had not yet launched an attack, this could happen at any moment. The Chinese had taken Nanking yesterday afternoon and committed some atrocities there. British and American warships had provided covering fire between the escaping European refugees and the communist soldiers, which finally allowed all the refugees to be brought on board the warships. Some had been wounded and others had broken their limbs when the sheets they had been using to slide down the walls of Nanking had broken, and no one knew exactly what was going to happen next. We had to retrieve Director Jones from Tungchow and take him to Chinkiang[8] and then receive new orders from the American destroyer.

8   Zhenjiang

Then the manager asked *Mei Hsia's* captain, Miclo, if he would risk going without an escort, because no one knew what might happen and the Chinese also had cannons, to which he replied that he would go.[9] Then I was asked the same question. I replied that I would go but as I was a family man, I asked them to please look after my family and to try and send them back to our homeland in the event that something should happen to me. This they promised to do. Then the manager wished us a good trip and we returned to our ships and I sailed out right away, hoping that *Mei Hsia* would follow me. He was delayed for a while, however, and I moved ahead at low speed. By the time I left the Whangpoo River and reached the Yangtze, I finally saw *Mei Hsia* behind me and we began our journey upriver. As we approached Vine Point, I saw a Chinese cruiser anchored in the middle of the river giving signals. I reduced speed and tried to read the signals but I didn't understand them and thought it was probably a Chinese army code. I wasn't sure what to do next. Who did the cruiser belong to, the communists or the central government? I nonetheless decided to sail to the ship and ask if I could pass through.

And so I went and asked. The reply was that I could but that the communists were at Vine Point and we needed to be careful.

I kept going. *Mei Hsia* had already caught up to me and now we went ahead together, reaching Vine Point and then passing by it. Not a single shot was fired at us but we saw soldiers on land, and on the previous day *Mei Hsia* had taken a lot of fire. As it was now evening, we decided to drop anchor four miles below the port of Tungchow, and at daylight the next morning to send ashore the wheelman from a small motorboat whom we had brought with us from Shanghai because he knew Tungchow.

---

9   Joe Miclo was a Yangtze River ship captain for Standard Oil who was ultimately dismissed by the Company after an altercation with a pilot.

He was to deliver a letter to the nearest Chinese agent, directing him to find Mr. Jones and to make telephone contact with the other agents. And we did just that. Our ships were alongside each other, the *Mei Hsia* with its anchor dropped, and my ship was on his left. We waited like this until 4 p.m. in the afternoon. Then the wheelman returned with Mr. Jones and we were able to continue our journey.

Because the forts in Kiangyin[10] were forty miles upriver and could probably already be in the hands of the communists, while the northern bank was still controlled by the central government's forces, we were afraid to sail through at night because one side or the other might start shooting at us with their cannons. So, we dropped anchor twenty miles below the forts, among some islands, where the river was very wide and it was difficult for soldiers to get close to us. We met a British passenger ship there that had dropped anchor before us to wait, as occasionally a British warship would come by and, if so, would take them past the forts. The other captain and I discussed what we should do as the river was only a half to one mile wide near the forts, and although the Chinese — the central government's soldiers — were poor shots, this did not mean that the communists also shot poorly. Further, the communist cannon units included Russian communists and areas near the forts on the south bank were already under the communists' control.

We decided to proceed nonetheless and early the next morning we began our journey. The British ship could travel at 14 knots and it went first. *Mei Hsia*, which could go almost 16 knots, was in the middle and my ship, *Mei Tan*, which could travel at 17 knots, had no scow and went last. When we reached the closest point to the forts we were fired upon by cannons and guns. The bullets

---

10   Jiangyin

came in swarms, mainly targeting the first two ships, and I was only struck here and there. However, the shooting came from both banks and we took a beating from both the communists and from the central government. Seeing that our situation was poor I moved to full steam ahead, as did the others, and as my ship was faster I passed them. *Mei Hsia* also passed the British ship. That is how we got out of shooting range and waited for each other, asking if anyone had been injured. It became clear that bullets had struck us only here and there but a six-inch shell had landed on the deck of the British ship, smashing through the top deck and falling amongst the passengers on the second deck, where three people had been injured. Fortunately, the shell didn't explode.

We kept going. In several places guns from the riverbank shot at us, until we met a large British cruiser leading a convoy of a dozen ships down to Shanghai. Its decks were filled to overflowing with Europeans and Americans, from Nanking and elsewhere. They advised us that an American destroyer was ahead, also coming downriver, and was waiting for us at the next fort until we passed.

The wounded from the British ship were transferred onto the cruiser to be taken to Shanghai.

We then found ourselves facing the American destroyer, which advised that it had taken fire when passing the fort on Silver Island. One shell had pierced the deck beside the bridge and had fallen through to the officers' mess but it hadn't exploded and no one had been injured. They also said they had turned back and fired on the fort with all of their side cannons and that the cannons in the fort were unusually exposed, and they had seen many of them flying up in the air when their shells had landed. In any case, after this they had not fired any more shells and we should not be afraid because another destroyer was in

Chinkiang. It would guard us while we were there and would keep its cannons trained at the fort while we came through the narrows, in case they let off even one shot.

We arrived in Chinkiang without any unusual happenings. Mr. Jones remained behind there on one of our Company's motor yachts that was alongside the destroyer. The yacht's living quarters were equipped with all the comforts, even bathtubs.

We received an order to sail on to Nanking, and were advised that nothing unusual had happened recently and that all white people had either gone to Shanghai or were living aboard passenger ships under the protection of warships, down on the Middle River.

Since it was only 47 miles from Chinkiang to Nanking, we arrived there just before nightfall and were directed to come alongside the American Admiral's ship. A few miles below Nanking, a Japanese destroyer under full steam passed very close by *Mei Tan*. As *Mei Tan* was similar in design to an American tug and sat quite low in the water, only a few feet above the waterline, and although the command bridge was 6 feet higher than the deck, the ship disappeared completely under 6-7 feet of water and even the bridge deck was covered in a foot of water. I thought that this time things had come to an end but the ship bobbed up again and we emerged from the wash. However, all the cabins were full of water and the engine room had two feet of water. The mechanic had been able to close the hatch to the boiler room so although some water flowed in there from the engine room, very little water came from the top and the fires stayed lit.

The captain of *Mei Hsia*, who had sailed on *Mei Tan* for years, knew the ship and when the Japanese destroyer had passed by him, he stopped to see what would happen to *Mei Tan*. He later said that at one point he could only see the top of the smokestack so he thought that we were sinking to the bottom, and he took over the wheel of his ship to come and see if there were still a few of us he could save. He had, however, seen the bridge came out of the water and then, like some kind of water buffalo, the entire *Mei Tan* followed, sputtering and shaking. Miraculously, none of the crew had been hurt. After I had seen the destroyer creating the wave, I had shouted for everyone to run for cover and they had all made it into the shelter, as the crew was experienced and had worked on this ship for a long time and knew its features.

After staying in Nanking for one night we received an order that *Mei Hsia* was to go to Kiukiang[11] and to take direction from the manager there, and I was to go to Wuhu. We left Nanking at 3 in the morning and arrived in Wuhu at 9 in the morning, which was only 52 miles upriver, and *Mei Hsia* had another 197 miles to go upriver.

In the spring of 1927, I went to Wuhu with the ship to stand by the storage depot. We had a dozen depots downriver. The women — Europeans — were sent away, but the supervisor of the stores and other officials who needed to guard the stores stayed there, and if an incident took place then everyone was to come on board the ship. In an emergency, the ship went alongside the American gunboat that was at anchor in the middle of the river. Between Shanghai and Hankow there were about 20 destroyers, some gunboats and one cruiser on the river. In Shanghai, however, there sat many cruisers and destroyers.

Now I'll discuss a specific incident. In the office at the depot we had 60,000 Chinese silver dollars (about $20,000 American dollars) in a box that was kept in the safe. It was necessary to retrieve this, though, as it was expected that Chiang Kia-shek was coming with his forces. The 5,000 soldiers in Wuhu might start to revolt, destroy our building and steal the money. But

---

11   Jiujiang

there were only four of us, all Caucasians — the manager, the supervisor of the stores, a mechanic and myself. The other three were Americans and I was Estonian. The American gunboat was nearby but didn't want to trouble itself with this matter. Others wondered if I had enough courage to bring the silver onto the ship.

I took the ship to a wharf below the city and then went with the manager to the office. The manager and the Chinese loaded the money into boxes, with $1,500 into each box. I then assigned two pair of Chinese to carry each load. Using bamboo yokes each pair of Chinese carried two boxes between them. Thus we went from the office onto the ship. I had two revolvers in my pocket and the Chinese went ahead with the silver and I followed behind. It was ¼ mile to the ship and Chinese soldiers were everywhere, along the side of the road and elsewhere. I made 10 return trips like this. It was open ground from the office to the ship. Every soldier watched us, however no one dared to do anything. The mechanic again kept guard with a revolver on the ship's deck. At last we sailed from below the city to beside the American destroyer, which was two miles below the city, and loaded all the money onto it. Despite the fact that I had not been afraid, after the stress involved with this work I was nevertheless in a state of nervousness.

The money was to be returned to the Chinese bank in five days. By then the situation had changed. No longer were there any ravaging soldiers and it was more peaceful. Chiang Kai-shek was in power. I alone took the money back ashore but then there was no longer any danger.

China is rife with counterfeit money and I have to say that it has all been skillfully reproduced. A Chinese pilot, with whom I was already acquainted, once came onto my ship. He had frequently been a pilot aboard my ship for 3-4 years. He complained that he did not have enough money to buy food and asked me to loan him a few dollars.

I didn't happen to have any money on me but as I still wanted to help the man, I borrowed 8 Chinese dollars from my Norwegian First Mechanic that I then gave to the Chinaman. Two days afterwards the Chinaman repaid his loan and I passed the money on to the mechanic. The mechanic looked at the money and said that unfortunately it was counterfeit. I reprimanded the Chinaman and asked if he wasn't ashamed to repay a loan, from someone who trusted him, with forged money, but he only smirked.

Because of gambling, some families had nothing to eat for months. The Chinese on the ship also always gambled, playing mahjong or Chinese card games. The game continued until one person ended up with all the money.

It used to be that white men beat up the Chinese, but this was later forbidden. It sometimes happened, though, that a dispute led to fighting and then the Chinese would use the blows inflicted upon them by a white man to blackmail him for a few dollars.

One time, at four o'clock in the morning, my crew started quarreling with one another. They were beating each other bloody and I was unable to just calmly watch this brawl. So, to bring an end to it, I decided to wade in with a few blows. One clever man, who had received a weak blow to the body, took advantage of this right away and pressed some money from me for the pain.

In March, the American government gave the order that all Americans above Hankow were to evacuate. No longer were there any ships to provide protection. All the white families above Hankow left and came downriver, leaving not a single white person upriver. There were only a few whites left in Chungking, namely a couple of Germans. In the presence of the American Consul and the Chinese government, all storage facilities in Chungking were sealed. The officials were called away and they all left and came down river.

In August 1927, I was assigned to another ship, *Mei Hsia*, which was one year old and had the most powerful engines of any ship on the river. She was a tanker of almost 1,000 tons. In addition, *Mei Hsia* had been built using the latest construction techniques and had all the conveniences — refrigeration and distillation units, etc.

In China, one still had to distill bath water to get rid of the bugs in it and this was done with the help of Lysol.[12] Otherwise, all types of skin diseases could be contracted, which could not be treated with any kind of doctoring. This ship, however, had a water distillation unit. With *Mei Hsia*, I went above Hankow where I needed to deliver oil products to the cities that needed them. Our business method had now changed. Previously, the Company delivered products to warehouses and storage depots and the agents made their purchases and took ownership of the goods there. Now the Company effectively sold products downriver and a Company ship delivered them where needed.[13]

This was a very dangerous time as there was no protection but there were many bandits. On my ship there were but two Europeans, the mechanic and I, and we needed to be vigilant at all times. The crew could generally be trusted, but in case of an emergency we didn't expect them to be of any help. The bandits were mainly on land, however.

At night we weren't able to sail at all. The ship was anchored

---

12 Lysol, a common disinfectant, has been produced for over 100 years. During the 1918 Spanish flu pandemic it was promoted as an effective way to kill the influenza virus.

13 The changes likely were because Standard Oil wished to improve its position relative to its Chinese agents under American and international laws, focusing on where title to goods passed hands and which party held certain responsibilities.

in the middle of the river where the current was the strongest. In daytime we could go and tie up at the town jetty, but at night we had to anchor in the river again. British, American, French and Japanese warships sat at anchor near the city of Hankow.

We sailed like this the entire winter. Sometimes we sailed together with a few other ships. In the evenings we fastened our ships to one another for extra safety.

Until the spring of 1928, I sailed under God's love and care and by then the situation had improved and six new American warships, which the U.S. government was providing for our protection, were ready. Our office reopened the upper storage depots and began to trade through them.

All of us — four ships at once — went together to Chungking with two American warships, one in front and the other behind. Even the Admiral and his staff came with us and he stayed on my ship. Our General Manager from Shanghai was also along and a director from New York. They were staying on the *Mei Ping*.

Arriving in the city of Wanhsien, half way between Ichang and Chungking, a revolution was about to break out as the communists were coming. As we arrived late at night, we had to stay in Wanhsien. We were nervous of course, but there was nowhere else to go.

The entire night, we heard gunfire in the distance and the forces defending the city were able to repulse the attackers.

In the spring of 1928 before sailing to Chungking, our three ships went for a test run to Ichang under the protection of an American gunboat, to see what the conditions were like. Arriving at Ichang, the gunboat stayed 1½ miles below the city. One ship dropped anchor and two of us went and tied up at the wharf by our storage depot. In the evening, a message arrived that bandits were coming and wanted to rob the ship. At first we didn't want to believe this because of the presence of the American gunboat and the other gunboats. The Chinese however, confirmed that bandits were coming and that they were always well-informed. We prepared for a fight without saying anything to the captain of the gunboat, because it was possible that no bandits would show up.

On my ship were myself, a Russian First Officer and an American First Mechanic. On the other ship, the Captain and the First Officer were Latvians and the First Mechanic was an American, who had gone to visit his friend on the ship that had dropped anchor. Thus, five of us stayed aboard the two ships. We let down all the steel shutters, loaded our rifles and put a watch outside. On the wharf, we set up some searchlights so that no one could sneak up on us, and then we waited. We thought that if they came we would turn on our siren, which the gunboat would then hear and come to help us. After 10 p.m. heavy gunfire began at the southern end of our storage depot, a proper battle that lasted for twenty minutes. We saw people running and falling. A patrol of soldiers from the city had run into the bandits — whether or not they knew about the planned attack or if their meeting was accidental, we don't know. They defeated the bandits, many of whom were killed, and a few men from the patrol also died but we did not have to fire a single shot. We kept watch for the rest of the night but weren't bothered. The next morning, about thirty bodies could be seen on the riverbank. When the American gunboat heard about this incident it came to the depot right away and remained there and didn't go below the city any more.

The situation improved the next year because Chang Kai-shek changed his politics. He paid off the Russians and sent them away, and restored order, although he rejected the Bolshevik regime that had been in place for over a year. Bandits remained everywhere, though. We were able to sail only when we had soldiers aboard or an American gunboat as an escort. The gunboats escorted us for four months. This was very troublesome however, and also expensive. Sometimes up to ten ships were together as the gunboats wouldn't come for just one or two ships, and we still had to find an anchorage with room for all of the ships. One gunboat went in front and another at the rear, and as one ship was not allowed to be within 500 yards of another, and even this was hazardous, the convoy was so long that you could not see the other end and those ships not visible to the gunboats were hit by gunfire from the riverbank.

The gunboat escorts were finally discontinued and then sailors were placed onboard every ship. This was still the practice when I left there, and remains the practice today on the Upper River. Sometimes the accompanying sailors came from Hankow and sometimes from Ichang, bringing their own munitions with them. Each ship was provided with four to six sailors and one officer.

Even on the Middle River between Hankow and Ichang it was dangerous during these years, although not as bad as on the Upper River. The opposite bank on the Middle River, beginning thirty miles above Hankow and continuing upriver, was in the hands of the communists. Chang Kia-shek was at war with the communists for 5-6 years.

In the fall of 1928, before Christmas, my wife and daughter came from Shanghai to visit me and afterwards they were to travel back to our homeland. Because living conditions in Hankow were very poor and because I was going to be on the Upper River again during the summer, there was no benefit for them to stay there. Before Christmas I was ordered to go 130 miles upriver. As I wished to spend Christmas with my family, I took my wife and daughter along, even though we had no protection because this was provided only on the Middle River.

Arriving in Chenglin, where the ship was cleared to proceed, the Chinese customs officer mentioned to me that there were many bandits in the area. I needed to sail another five miles upriver to the town of Yochow [Yueyang] on the bank of Tung Ting Lake [Dongting Lake], where things were even worse. Because there was not a single European in Chenglin, I didn't want to leave my wife and eight-year-old daughter ashore where there was no protection aside from the odd Chinese soldier, so they remained on the ship.

When we arrived at the other port, everything seemed to be in order. It was a walled town and the gates were closed at night. We anchored below the town and waited to see what might happen. Onboard were the mechanic and I, both Europeans, and of course my wife and daughter. The conditions were poor. It wasn't possible to go to another place, as it could be even worse. We planned to fight back, if necessary, and we readied our firearms, lowered the steel shutters and kept watch all night. I showed my wife how to load the rifle and revolver and explained to her that if I was killed she had to first shoot our daughter and then kill herself. While the situation was dangerous, fortunately no bandits came to attack us. A few days later though, a Spanish priest came from across the lake and was murdered.

After returning to Hankow my wife and daughter sailed to Shanghai and from there went back to our homeland. Thereafter, the situation improved every year. Chiang Kai-shek achieved control over almost all of China, from the Yangtze valley to Chungking, while the war with the communists steadily continued. The communists came to the edge of the river, robbed European ships and took their captains ashore, demanding outrageously large ransoms for their release. Some people had been held captive for up to six months. The robbing of people had occurred a lot more frequently before there were any new American gunboats, but also afterwards if there were no soldiers aboard a ship.

We went about our chores and kept to ourselves, because if people were seen moving about on a ship, the Chinese were afraid to come. They preferred to approach stealthily, which is why it was necessary to keep a watch. In general, there was continuous shooting on the river — fights between sailors and bandits. We shone searchlights on the riverbank at night to make it was hard for us to be seen but we were able to see everything. Of course, we were fired upon from the bank but we had better opportunities to return fire. The ship also had its protective plates in place during the day but these were secured only on one side, as fastening them on both sides would have made it too hot. It was dangerous nonetheless as the sound made by the river current often made it difficult to hear anything on the command bridge until shells were in the air, and only then was it possible to know which side the shots were coming from.

Many people died because of this. A British captain was killed, a mechanic on my ship received a bullet in his leg and is suffering to this day, and five men were killed at one time on a Japanese ship.

All in all, sailing the Upper River, particularly the 350 miles between Ichang and Chungking, was one of the most difficult trips for a captain. For example, during the summer there is a fast current, rocks, rapids, large fluctuations in water level, poor places to anchor and only a few places large enough to anchor up to seven ships. It is never possible to be sure that a particular place is a good one as it all depends on the water level. If a place to drop anchor cannot be found, then the ship must be fastened to rocks using spears, which are twisted into cracks, and the ship is then secured with cables to the spears, which keeps the ship away from the rocks. Sailing is possible only during the daytime and at night the ship must be at anchor. In the summer, it was already light at 3:30 in the morning and we needed to sail until 8:30 in the evening — 18 hours. After the anchors have been weighed and the ship is underway, it is steered by a pilot. Everything else is up to the captain: being aware of all signals, choosing a place to anchor and then doing so, regulating the speed, yielding to other ships where required, making sure no junks are swamped, supervising the pilot and ensuring he doesn't fall asleep, deciding when to fight with bandits, etc.

Chinese pilots are generally good but they take many risks, more than any white man would dare to take, and every year up to 40% of ships suffer by being completely wrecked or sustaining damages.

If a ship is powerful — I had one of the most powerful ships, it was oil-fueled and had 4,000 h.p. — then the ship can make it through all places without any heaving. However, there was one place with a water depth of 68 ft. where heaving was not possible. If the water level rose above 68 ft. all ships had to stop until the water level decreased.

The river has large fluctuations in water level, and water can rise up to the 275 ft. level in the gorges. I have not sailed at a level greater than 160 ft. When the water rose I waited for it to start falling. Only once I went when the water was at 165 ft. and the entire time I had to race ahead at full steam to be able to steer the ship, and several times I thought that we would smash against the rocks.

When the water is rising, the river changes. In the gorges, the water piles up to quite a height and then there is nowhere to secure a ship. The gorges are quite lengthy, being 2½, 3, 4½, 14 and 24 miles long.

One ship was lost without anybody knowing where, though

usually it was always known where a ship was going and if and where it had been wrecked. This happened in 1930. The ship left in the morning and disappeared. There was a place where round boulders had accumulated since the ice ages and it was necessary to sail through these for over twenty miles. The water rises and runs over the boulders and if a ship strikes the rocks it will get wrecked. There is a channel but if the pilot makes an error then the ship will go to the bottom. The Chinese are very clever, though, and can perceive rocks to a depth of 8-10 feet from how the river is flowing.

Due to the rocks, a ship with 80 passengers onboard was once wrecked. The number of people on a Chinese ship is never reported accurately because there are always stow-a-ways on board. Similarly wrecked was a ship with 300 passengers.

Sixty people were once killed aboard a passenger ship because bandits were shooting at it. The passengers did not have any protection and ran below the deck, but everyone was not able to make it because Chinese put too many people aboard each ship. There have been occasions when bandits get control of an entire ship and then it can be seen how a European ship starts shooting at other ships. In Europe such an incident would have had political repercussions, but here where bandits are commonplace it is an everyday occurrence.

Ships help each other when they pass by providing information, if they have any, about the location of bandits. There are wooden notice boards for this, upon which messages are written in chalk such as "Bandits on the right at mile so and so" etc. The other ship then knows when to be ready. Many ships write a note if they cannot pass through, and sometimes it happens that one ship is unable to get through but another one comes and passes through. The worst, however, is coming to anchor in the evening, getting a message that bandits are nearby, and then trying to move to another place but finding no better spot to anchor in and just having to wait there, come what may. It is also not surprising if ships have many bullet holes. I have seen two ships with all their paint shot off. The people went down to the bottom of the hull for shelter because the bullets thoroughly pierced the upper structure of the ship. One time, a hole was shot in the ballast tank of my ship. I have also been under fire for up to half an hour. Three men were wounded and one, the pilot, died. It was a perpetual battleground on the river, sometimes up to three fights in one day.

The worst is when there are bandits near rapids, because then nothing can be done but to turn back. Going up rapids is especially slow when you do not have enough power to get through and you have to heave. This, of course, cannot be done and you have to go back.

To sail on the Upper River, you need very strong nerves and a thorough knowledge of your ship, and you also have to be able to think quickly to decide what to do in each situation.

In addition to government officials, professionals and other positions of status in China, bandits or robbers play an important role, and this has been a Chinese occupation for millennia. In reality, there is very little difference between a Chinese soldier and a robber. If somewhere you see a man wearing what looks like a soldiers' uniform then you should always keep your distance, because you can never be sure if he is a soldier or a robber. Often the same person frequently switches occupation between a soldier and a robber, and you can never tell which he happens to be at the moment.

Robbers frequently gather in large gangs to occupy and terrorize entire communities and towns, levying payments to themselves from the communities. This continues until a stronger gang of robbers comes along to take over their power and their payments.

Generally, every Chinaman is ready to rob, whereas bandits are those Chinese who earn their living only by robbing.

When robbers are fortunate enough to capture a ship they will strip it bare, kill the crew and take the officers captive, holding them in a jail until they are able to collect a ransom from their families. If no money is forthcoming from relatives, then an ear, finger or hand is sent to them, and if this does not result in a payment then the prisoner is killed.

In this fashion, some robbers received a ransom of 45,000 American dollars, 30 gold wristwatches, 150 hats and 130 winter coats for a British Navy Reserve captain who they were holding hostage.

Trains were also robbed and white passengers were taken prisoner and held for ransom. One time, in this fashion, a number of important foreigners were captured. Chinese authorities sent the army to capture the robbers and to free the whites, but this attempt failed. The Chinese government was left with no alternative but to try and reach an agreement with the robbers. In addition to receiving a ransom payment, the robbers received positions in the Chinese army - the leader of the robbers as an officer, and the other robbers as ordinary soldiers. Robbers are created primarily when generals fight against each other. They lose the ability to pay wages to their armies, who then begin to look after themselves by robbing.

On the river the robbers tended to attack ships by shooting from the riverbank with rifles, and also sometimes with shoddy frontloading cannons.

They sometimes attacked ships using their junks, but many of these were sunk and these types of attacks became rare. To protect against robbers, ships had steel shutters on the bridge that were lowered in emergencies. In addition, ships carried tear gas, automatic rifles, machineguns and Colt pistols. Gun battles between robbers and ships were an everyday occurrence. Sometimes the bands of robbers were very large. One time I saw a large band of robbers that numbered 4,500 men. The robbers were on one bank of the river and soldiers were on the other side. There was continuous shooting over our heads as we passed by.

Robbers were particularly troublesome on the Upper River. Sailing at night was not possible here as the rapids made it dangerous. When it was dark, ships either stayed at anchor or fastened themselves to the rocks with wires. Sometimes it was known that robbers were ahead, and when it was certain that the next anchorage could not be reached before darkness fell, it was crucial to remain where one was.

Attacks begin with shooting from the shore and when a ship no longer returns fire then the attackers row to the ship and try to board it. It is even worse if the bandits do not shoot from shore at all but try to reach the ships stealthily, in their boats, under the cover of darkness. Chinese helmsmen, who are usually left on night watch, cannot be relied upon because they are careless and fall asleep. This is why officers need to man the watch themselves.

Even so, pirates have captured many ships. The crews are killed or taken hostage and the ships are stripped bare (*of anything of value*) and are then set on fire. It is a perpetual war.

In 1928 the pirates had become so bold that soldiers from warships were stationed on merchant ships to provide protection against them.

It's unfortunate that due to the loud roar of the river, it is not possible to hear shots being fired from shore and to know that pirates are attacking until bullets are already whizzing over the ship.

The pirates secretly buy foreign ammunition and when it

runs out they make their own bullets and gunpowder.

Sometimes soldiers also shoot at ships, to try and force the ships to pick them up and take them elsewhere.

Onetime, on the Upper River, I had two American Admirals along as passengers, and also the Secretary of the Embassy, and the Consul and his wife. Suddenly, an oncoming ship gave notice that pirates were nearby so we lowered the steel shutters and arranged ourselves in a defensive position, just as heavy shooting at us started from the riverbank. We returned fire and it became a pandemonium, with crackling and smoke everywhere. The women fainted. The Admirals looked grave, and later told us they would not have believed that the situation here was so bad.

In August 1930, when I was on *Mei Hsia*, the communists invaded from Fukien Province, through Kiangsi Province to Hunan Province and its capital city of Changsha. This was one of the wealthiest places in the land, with fertile farmlands, valuable minerals such as antimony, zinc, copper, tin, and coal, and more to be found. Changsha is a city of over two million people located on the banks of the Siankiang River. The Siankiang River runs into the Yangtze River 129 miles above Hankow. During the high water levels of summer, river ships of up to 3,000-tons can sail there, but in the winter there is only 1-2 feet of water in some places and then it is only possible to travel along the river in a small boat. Changsha is 93 miles upstream from the mouth of this river — where the Siankiang runs into the Yangtze River.

When I came to Hankow from the Upper River with a load, I received an order to, when I was ready, sail directly to Changsha without stopping, the same as all other ships that were available. Accordingly, I hurried to Changsha where I arrived the next day. The communists had already done their work here but the exchange of gunfire could still be heard. When the communists had begun their attack, the Governor of Hunan along with the head of the army, believing their forces were not strong enough, had evacuated to the other side of the river leaving the city undefended to face the communists. The attackers began to steal, murder and burn in a frightful fashion, capturing all the wealthy Chinese and torturing them to get whatever money, gold and other valuables any of them had. In the first few days, the communists murdered and tortured over 2,000 of the stoutest and wealthiest Chinese. It is known that Chinese methods of torture are extremely barbaric but those of the communist Chinese were even worse and I do not want to write about this here because it would be too difficult.

The Europeans and Americans, who lived on a small island in the middle of the river where only white people and the Japanese lived, had been sent away earlier. The merchants lived either on gunboats or beside them on motor yachts, which is why nothing happened to them. In the city, two Germans had barricaded themselves in a well-built stone building and they also had good revolvers with them. The communists had tried to get them but ran short of time and were not successful in doing so. After being under siege for two days the Germans emerged unharmed.

Gunboats were at anchor only 1½ miles below the city, however they didn't want to interfere. The next morning, the Italian gunboat pulled up to the city to see if somehow it could find a couple of Catholic priests who had not yet arrived from outside of the city. When the ship came in line with the city, the communists began firing at them from shore, and then the ship fired back with all of its armaments. The other gunboats — American, British and two Japanese — saw that a fight had broken out and weighed anchor to come to the aid of the Italian ship, and so five gunboats had their cannons blazing against the rifles of the communists, who started to panic and, fearing that the Europeans would also send forces ashore, began a retreat and ran out of the city.

The Chinese general and his forces had become bolder and had also started to attack the communists from across the river, and when I arrived there were battles going on near the city. As communists were still in some buildings alongside the river, shooting onto the river with their guns at whomever they saw, we had to remain at anchor on the river where there was protection. We received orders to evacuate all our oil supplies and oil products to Hankow, because not one gunboat had been able to go downstream from Changsha since November due to the low water level. To remain there would have been very dangerous because if the communists returned they might damage the gunboats and all would be lost. To leave the oil supplies there without any gunboats would have been very risky, so I made five trips from Hankow to Changsha along with our five other ships. We emptied all the stores, and our employees also left, leaving only a few guards for the now-empty depot.

Because the communists had reached the river's edge in many places and life had become dangerous for the missionaries, we picked up many missionary families from the riverbanks — children, women and men — of various nationalities and religious denominations, and took them to Hankow with us.

8

BATTLES BETWEEN THE CHINESE AND
THE JAPANESE IN 1932

IN RECENT YEARS the Chinese people have become much more cultured. Many European schools have been established and missionary organizations have helped. This education has shown good results and after finishing school, those Chinese who can afford it, go to America, England or Germany to attend university. The Chinese will graduate with a degree but are ineffectual at actually working and cannot seem to accomplish anything. However, this may also hold true about Europeans these days.

I believe that the Japanese will not succeed in their war against China, as all of China is up in arms. The land is without roads and is difficult to move around in. To take control they would have to conquer all of China, which they could never do. They tempt the Chinese though, by promising to install a Chinese ruler and they believe that the Chinese will give in, but they will not. The Japanese will not be able to do anything more, and if they enter into a treaty of any kind they will have lost anyhow. They will have no choice but to continue the war, and the longer it goes on the more harmful it will be for Japan.

At the beginning of February 1932, I came to Shanghai with *Mei Foo*, which needed repairs. As my wife had sailed from our homeland to China in November 1931, she was traveling with me. When we arrived in Shanghai the conflict between the Chinese and the Japanese had already begun, but hadn't turned into fighting yet. After we reached the wharf at our supply depot, ten Japanese destroyers arrived in Shanghai and moored themselves on some buoys upriver from us. My wife was planning to go ashore, but the depot manager advised that fighting between the Chinese and the Japanese could start at any moment and, if it did, it was uncertain whether she could make it back to the ship. Accordingly, we decided it was best not to visit the city then but that the next day, if possible, we would both go.

During the night, or more properly early the next morning, Japanese from the Hongkou part of the city had pushed into the Chinese town of Chapei, where there were Chinese soldiers, and fighting began immediately. The ship did not have up-to-date reports but as streetcars, cars and buses were moving, we planned to go ashore. We went to the office and were advised that the ship was being overhauled right away, that the work had already begun, and that it needed to be completed urgently.

We left the ship and went to town, where I met an acquaintance. I asked him how things were going in the city, because no one knew anything but the fighting was continuing. He said that he had just come from North Szechuen Road and that the Japanese had initially made good progress, though the Chinese had fought back well using the shelter of buildings and had finally begun to counterattack. As there were only 2,000 Japanese, they weren't able to provide much resistance to this and things were becoming more complicated. All of Shanghai's volunteer soldiers were already at their posts on the boundaries between the different sections of the city, and the Chinese were only attacking the Japanese and not harming the Europeans or the Americans.

Because the noise of cannons and machineguns was getting louder, my wife and I decided to try and get back to the ship right away. We took a taxi and began our journey. Arriving at the railway bridge over Soochow Creek there were so many people, cars and all kinds of wagons that we weren't able to get through and we had to stop on the bridge in all the traffic. A Chinese cannon shell had exploded right beside the bridge, as the Chinese had begun to fire their cannons, from the other side of the city, at the Japanese consulate and at the Japanese Admiral's ship that was stationed nearby. However, the Chinese were unable to direct fire onto their targets and their shells missed by up to one-quarter of a mile, which is how we came under fire.

The taxi driver did not go any further. Even though no one was able to move at first, we got out of the car nonetheless, pushed ourselves through the wall of people and made it to the other side of the bridge where there was already more room. We looked for another taxi but there were none to be found. We boarded a streetcar but this only took us a few kilometers and no further because there already was some shooting ahead. We then began to go on foot, keeping close to the walls of buildings, and in many places there were patrols of Japanese soldiers and city police, but all the same there was no shooting. We finally made it to the edge of the riverbank opposite the storage depot, where there was a telephone that connected with the depot. I wanted to summon a motorboat but the telephone line was disconnected.

A strong wind was blowing and it was also cold, and because of this we did not want to take a Chinese sampan over the river and we just waited to see what would happen.

After a short while, a car from the office arrived there with the depot manager and his wife, who had ordered a motorboat by telephone. So, after a three-hour adventure we finally arrived back at the ship. Fighting was now going on day and night but although the Japanese destroyed Chapei with their cannons they were still were unable to move ahead. Each day brought more and more Japanese soldiers and their warships, and the tumult of war continued night and day. The thunder from cannon-fire was so loud that it was only possible to sleep in fifteen-minute intervals with all the racket going on. Chapei was burning and at night this left a dreadful impression. Every time the cannon batteries fired the ship would shudder and shake so much that we became afraid. We had already taken the engine apart when I received an order to be ready to leave in 24 hours. So we had to reassemble everything and build up our steam without having had time to make any repairs.

I received an order to load gasoline for Chinkiang [Zhenjiang] and Nanking, and after arriving in Nanking to make myself available to the manager there. It was possible that the ship would stay in Nanking for some time and that the workers there, and their families, might come and live on board. It was also possible that their families had already been sent to Shanghai.

When the ship was loaded I left for Chinkiang. The previous day, five Japanese cruisers at anchor in the Yangtze River, 4-6 miles downriver from the mouth of the Whangpoo River, had shelled the fortresses of Woosung that were at the mouth of the Whangpoo River. These forts were shelled many times each day and foreign cargo ships were allowed to pass in-between, but only during the daytime. As soon as we were able to sail two or three miles towards the river mouth, the cruisers began to fire shells overland at the Woosung forts, the railway station, and other places. A large Norwegian steamship sailing in front of me turned around, and a British steamship did the same. My ship shuddered from the shell-fire. Then, three Japanese destroyers came towards me at full steam. They were under heavy machinegun fire from land and they returned fire using their cannons and machineguns. When we approached the first destroyer they shouted that it would be better if we turned around, because it presently was not possible to pass through.

So we turned around, as did the three other ships behind me. The other ships dropped anchor almost four miles from the river mouth, while I sailed back to our storage depot because those had been my orders. I saw how shells from the cruisers exploded among the buildings on land and blew them up. At the storage depot, I received an order to wait until tomorrow and not to leave without the manager's approval. None of the other ships returned and I figured that before nightfall, when things were more peaceful, they likely had been able to leave.

Later, however, I heard that just as the other ships were leaving the Whangpoo river mouth, shells from the cruisers had destroyed the radio broadcast station, which was on the riverbank, and shrapnel had reached the command bridge of the Norwegian ship and had smashed some things there, but miraculously no one had been hurt.

The next morning many ships left. Things were quiet and I asked if I too could leave. I finally received permission to go. The manager had feared that if I happened into a shooting, my cargo of gasoline might ignite and explode from the large changes in air pressure caused by exploding shells. When I left, I was the last ship to leave and the others were already out of sight, but I was still able to leave the Whangpoo River before the shooting started again. But now the shooting was behind my stern and as I was already farther away from land, the ship was no longer affected by exploding shells. Thus, I was able to reach Chinkiang, where I unloaded part of my cargo and then sailed on to Nanking.

When we arrived there, I heard that the women and children had already been sent to Shanghai. I was ordered to unload and then to wait and see what would happen next. Everything was quite quiet in Nanking. A few days earlier, three Japanese cruisers stationed below Nanking had begun to fire on the city at night, for no apparent reason, and everyone had been in a panic. It was because of this that I had been sent to Nanking.

After a few days in Nanking I received an order to sail back to Shanghai and I entered the Whangpoo River near Woosung just as a battle was going on between the Japanese and the Chinese. The Japanese were attacking Woosung's forts. The wooden bridge over the creek in Woosung was burning, as the Chinese had set it on fire to hinder the Japanese approach. The entire riverbank was filled with Japanese, lying down or running and attacking, and shooting their weapons. Bullets struck our hull and flew everywhere around the Japanese, but we were all under cover and sped by under full steam and arrived at our wharf without any injuries. I stayed with the ship again for its overhaul and the entire time the war was raging, until the evening of March 8th, when suddenly it became quiet, as though a large storm had passed.

My wife and I went to sleep early that evening, at 8 o'clock, and I awoke at 9 the next morning on the same side I had lain down on. I had slept for 12 hours without waking a single time, and so had my wife, as the clamor of war and the sounds of shellfire had tired us greatly over the weeks.

9

MORE PEACEFUL TIMES

AFTER 1932, the situation slightly improved. The number of bandits declined and there was no more shooting from the riverbank during the daytime, although shooting still occurred at night.

I sailed like this until 1935 and then went to my homeland again for a holiday, for the third time. I traveled via the Suez Canal, stayed until August, and then returned to China with my wife and youngest daughter via the Suez Canal.

The second time I had come via the Suez Canal on a Japanese passenger ship, and for the return trip to China I had traveled on *Karlsruhe*, a 16,000-ton Nord-Deutscher Lloyd passenger ship, to New York, then by train to San Francisco and from there to Shanghai on the Robert Dollar & Co. steamship line.

On my 1935 vacation, I sailed on *Kordiljera*, an 18,000-ton ship of the Hamburg-America Line, to Naples and then by rail to my homeland. Traveling by ocean liner is very comfortable and fun, especially on the American and German ships whose meals are also very good. I was always given a first-class ticket. I returned on a Dutch ship from Genoa to Shanghai, sailing back with my wife and daughter. They remained in Shanghai and I was placed on *Mei Ping*, which was one of our newest ships.

The office wanted to know which ship was better, *Mei Ping* or *Mei Hsia*, and I was put on board to evaluate her, because how good a ship was also depended on the captain. I thought that *Mei Hsia* was better, but the office thought otherwise.

During the winter of 1935/1936, I was on *Mei Lu* and in the spring of 1936, I went to try *Mei Ping*. I did not really want to go, because I had one more year to serve before retiring on December 31, 1937. However, I had to comply with the Company's order and so during the winter I sailed on *Mei Ping* and sometimes also on *Mei Lu*. In the spring when the water rose, I sailed on *Mei Ping*. This continued until the war broke out.

Until then, not a single one of my daughters or my wife had sailed on the Upper River. Previously, I had not wanted to show them this dangerous place because I was afraid they would be concerned and would start worrying about me. However, as I was going to be sailing there for the last time, I wanted to show it to them. Tourists from America and England paid a lot of money to see this dangerous part of the river.

My daughter went to school in a Catholic convent and in the spring when school was out, my wife and daughter came along on two trips from Hankow to Chungking, a distance of 740 miles. They were certainly afraid, as the water level was quite high. During the first trip, we waited in Ichang for five days because the water was too high — a level of 49 feet. Nonetheless, we sailed out early one morning. In the rapids the water almost pushed the ship on its side twice. My wife and daughter ran out to see what was going on, as they had still been asleep. It was early morning and a large thunder and roar could be heard. The sailing was very difficult and the entire day's progress was 90 miles upriver. The other ship, the one I had previously been on, fell behind and wasn't able to advance more than 65 miles and then dropped its anchor there. Our second trip also took place during the time of high water.

10

THE 1937 SINO JAPANESE WAR

THE WAR BEGAN in Peking in June 1937 when my family was aboard the ship. We did not pay any attention, believing that it was just the usual yearly small conflict between the Chinese and the Japanese. We arrived in Hankow on July 30th and I had already ordered tickets via telegraph for my family to go to Shanghai. We came into Hankow late that evening and their ship departed at 9:30 p.m. so there was only 1½ hours in between. I took my family to the passenger ship and they left for Shanghai.

This was the start of an adventure for my family. Their ship was hit by a large typhoon on the river between Hankow and Shanghai, and instead of reaching their destination in two days it took them five, because they anchored in several sheltered places to wait for the typhoon to pass. There are many different kinds of river ships and some are lightly built. My wife said that several times they were afraid that their ship would come apart.

They finally reached Shanghai on August 5, 1937. Shanghai was already gearing up for war, the Chinese were leaving the Japanese parts of town and the confusion was enormous. My wife and daughter could not even leave the ship because they couldn't get a taxi. The captain of their ship then telephoned my office, which sent the manager's car to pick them up. People were very agitated.

On August 13th fighting broke out in Shanghai. Chinese airplanes began bombing Japanese warships in the middle of the river, wanting to sink the Japanese Admiral's ship. The Japanese fired anti-aircraft cannons at the two Chinese planes, which caused the pilots to panic and they dropped their bombs onto their own city, into the busiest traffic, on Nanking Road and Avenue Edward VII.

One bomb fell on Nanking Road at one o'clock in the afternoon, which was good, because at that time most people, mainly officials, were at lunch and traffic was light. This is why the number of people killed was not very large — only a few hundred. If the incident had occurred at another time, either earlier or later in the day, when the office workers and officials were leaving their offices, the casualties would have been enormous.

The other airplane released its bombs onto the area of Avenue Edward VII where the streets were filled with Chinese refugees who had nowhere to go. More than 1,500 people were killed and 40 trucks were used to remove their remains.

My family was there during this time, until they left on August 24th. Almost all foreigners were evacuated, Americans, French, Italians, British, etc.

I lost communication with my family and did not know what had happened. The telegraph was not working and while the mail was moving, it was very slow and even telegrams were being sent by mail. An American warship provided a telegram saying the situation in Shanghai was very confusing, but I received no news about my family. Then I received a telegram from the office which said they had found space for my family on a ship and they were leaving on August 21st for San Francisco. I was asked for authorization to provide them with travel money in the amount of $300 and I gave this permission over an American warship's radio. I had told my wife to exchange all the money at the bank into English funds because I was going to be traveling back soon, and she had done so, but now all these funds were at the bank in my name and they did not have any cash to travel with.

A telegram arrived with the news that airplanes had bombed *President Hoover*, a passenger ship of the Robert Dollar Line, as it was entering the Yangtze River. The ship had to turn around because it sustained some damage and it was not coming back to Shanghai. No other American ships were coming either. Thus, my wife and daughter were unable to leave.

During the bombings, my wife had almost been killed while she was going to the bank. A bomb had fallen close by and a man, a European, had dragged her into a building for shelter. My wife, however, worrying about what was happening, wanted to rush home to see what was going on. She was finally able to get a rickshaw and sped home posthaste, where everything was fine.

The next day, my daughter had gone with Capt. Muusika's wife to go swimming at the YMCA swimming pool, which was downtown on Nanking Road. A bomb fell on a car twenty or thirty steps away from them, destroying it and killing the people inside. They then turned back, keeping close to the buildings and arrived home safely. After this, they did not dare to go outside again, and spent the day at home. They had also come down with malaria and were sick while at home.

The office then sent a message via the radio that Mrs. Mender was to come to the office to take care of some things, as passage had been secured for them on a French ship. A French warship would take them to the passenger ship and minimal luggage was to be taken along. The office also provided a car.

It was very crowded on the passenger ship and one of their suitcases, containing some valuables, was stolen.

My family sailed to Marseille and went from there to Paris, where the World's Fair was taking place, and in early October they arrived back in Estonia. The ship on which they had traveled was an old ship and had made many stops.

I had not known what was going on and had already sent airmail letters to relatives in San Francisco and New York saying that my wife and daughter were coming aboard the ship *President McKinley*, and asking to please keep them in America for a while so they could look around and forget the horrors they had witnessed here. Then, I suddenly received notice via radio that, according to the office, Captain Mender's wife and daughter were sailing to France aboard the French ship *Sphinx*, and I finally had some peace of mind.

I was on the Upper River, however. Finally there was nothing to transport as not a single tanker had been coming upriver when the conflicts began. We bought petroleum from Shell & Co. and also from Texas & Co., and provided them with other oil products that we had. We also bought gasoline and made trades with one another until finally there was nothing else to do.

At the end of October I took the ship out of service in Hankow so that it could be cleaned. The ship's officer that summer had been the Estonian, Captain P. Jakobson. He received an order to come to Shanghai, and was paid out there as he had only been on the payroll for the summer. I remained on the ship with the First Mechanic, who was an Italian, and eagerly waited for my retirement date, which was January 1, 1938. The Company wanted me to keep working but I was not interested, and they agreed to pay out my last salary. I began to worry about how I was going to leave China. I did not want to go by airplane because the way I saw it, traveling by airplane was still 99% more dangerous than sailing on the ocean, even though it would take only four hours travel by airplane to reach Hong Kong. Capt. Jakobson had flown to Hong Kong and praised the trip as being quite comfortable.

I was thinking of going to Chungking, and from there to Indo-China or to Burma, but permission for this trip was given only in exceptional circumstances because it was a very long route. I could have gone by taxi, but there were many bandits and because of this it would have been dangerous. The Chinese government always had to provide some protection along but did not want to do so for only a few travelers. Traveling by river wasn't possible because the river was closed to navigation. Most people traveled by airplane. Going on a junk would have been very dangerous as they would have shot me for being a spy, and even a letter from the office would not have helped. The end of my employment came closer each day and I did not know what to do. The office had not sent any messages.

Suddenly, I received orders that a ship was to come from Hankow to deliver supplies to the American and French warships and I was asked which ship it should be. I suggested *Mei Foo* but she did not run on oil. I was sure that if I went, I would not come back and would stay there until the retirement was formalized. I said my goodbyes and loading of my ship began. I left Hankow at 1 p.m. on November 18th and went to Wuhu, 52 miles above Nanking. No orders were waiting for me there and one ship, *Mei An*, was there at anchor. I continued on to Nanking where I arrived the same evening. The ship that had been stationed there was sent upriver to Hankow and I remained in its place. The manager came on board my ship and explained that I would stay there to provide the warships with oil and gasoline.

Everything from the stores was brought on board the ship, and all the staff came as well because the Japanese were getting closer. We gave oil to the French and American ships and some other people also came aboard the ship for shelter, as the Japanese were close by.

11

THE JAPANESE SINK USS PANAY IN A HAIL OF BOMBS.

ON OUR LAST EVENING there on December 6, when people were coming on board the ship, we heard the thunder of cannons and saw smoke. The captain of the American gunboat suggested that I should come within the protective range of the gunboats near the city, and so I did. I explained to him, however, and to my manager, that in my opinion, the most dangerous place was here between Pukow and Nanking, because when the Japanese airplanes came to drop bombs, shrapnel and debris might fall near us and, as the ship was filled with gas and oil, it would be better to be about three miles above Nanking where the British ships were. They finally agreed with me and I left with my ship. Because there were no American warships in Wuhu or Kingiung, our other ships, *Mei Hsia* and *Mei An*, also left the dangerous positions they had been in. They were going to take onboard some cargo that another ship had no room for. Similarly, all cutters and motor barges were summoned to Nanking and there were quite a few of these. Altogether, there were about fifteen British and American ships plus our small ships. We were under the protection of two British gunboats, HMS *Cricket* and HMS *Scarap*.

The USS *Panay*, the American gunboat, had to stay in the city, though, and could not leave until all Americans were aboard. However, there were sixteen missionaries and one reporter who did not want to leave and this is why *Panay* needed to stay, to take them on board if necessary. On my ship, in addition to myself and the mechanic, were three of the Company's managers, 113 Chinese — men, women and children — our personnel from many cities but mainly from Nanking, and the ship's crew of 45 men.

The entire time we were there, whenever the weather even barely allowed for it, Japanese airplanes came and bombed Nanking, which was on the south bank of the river, or Pukow, which was on the north bank of the river. When the alarm sounded, all foreign and Chinese ships, which were mainly passenger ships, left their wharfs to come and anchor near us. When the alarm was over, they returned to where they had been. If they had just begun to load when bombing started once more, they would leave again. Ships were able to work only during the night. All the Chinese who were able to left the city, and ships and junks were filled to the gunnels with people.

Because Japanese airplanes flew over us and were fired upon by Chinese anti-aircraft cannons, we always ran to take cover and frequently had bomb fragments fall onto the deck.

Bombing took place 4-6 times a day. Entire buildings were blown up and fires could be seen burning night and day. The last ships to leave toward Hankow left on the evening of December

8th. Only one very old Chinese steamship remained, which continuously carried soldiers across the river from Nanking to Pukow.

The cannon shells kept landing closer. From the ship's sundeck we were able to see munition depots being blown up and Nanking's southern gates being destroyed. Cannon fire ceased during the night, but began again early in the morning.

On December 9th, upriver from us along the riverbank, the Japanese shelled the city from close range. They had surrounded Nanking and then attacked from many sides with cannons and airplanes on December 9th, 10th and 11th. That afternoon we fled from there. On the morning of December 11th the only ship that remained there was anchored 1½ miles above Pukow.

On December 11th the Japanese bombed both Nanking and Pukow with airplanes and cannons. Large fires were burning everywhere, things were being blown up and the entire area seemed like a continuous sea of fire.

Around two o'clock in the afternoon we went up to the sundeck to watch Nanking being bombed. Suddenly, we heard the sound of a terrible explosion nearby. We looked and saw a column of smoke rising from beside a British ship. The ship was a bit behind us and was closer to the riverbank. We did not understand what was going on at first, until there was an explosion beside another ship. Then we realized that we were being bombed. I ran to the telegraph to send a message to the engine room to get the engine ready and ordered the anchor to be heaved. I received a quick reply that the engine was ready and we went full steam ahead, leaving the anchor to drag behind us. We began our escape under cannon-fire. All the ships weighed anchor and raced to the other side of the river and upriver. Bombs fell among us, although most of them fell on shore. Columns of smoke and waterspouts were everywhere. Two British ships were in front and bombs fell near them, which sent us scattering. I thought that we would not be able to get by and I slowed the engine. Then bombs fell not far from us. I moved into a forward gear again. We were bombed like this for 35 minutes. Then we went so far upriver that bombs couldn't reach us any more.

One bomb had exploded so close to a British ship that its entire left side was shattered and covered in bomb fragments. One man had been blown overboard and many men had been wounded. The ship began to sink but continued to move ahead to get out of firing range. By the time we had been able to leave the area, the ship had been steered to shallow water and a barge had been brought alongside it. The ship's cargo was transferred onto the barge, the hole in the ship's hull was patched and the ship was later salvaged. On the other British ship, two men had also been blown overboard and one was saved while the other drowned. The American ships were unharmed. While fleeing, we saw bombs falling on the city near *Panay*, where they created waterspouts. Then *Panay* also began to flee and followed us at full steam. When she passed us she signaled that we should anchor fourteen miles above Nanking. We arrived there just before nightfall and all of our ships anchored there. However, when the British ships finished their repairs and re-organized themselves, they went three miles above us to drop anchor.

At our previous anchorage, from where we had fled, there was a pontoon belonging to a British company that had no steam power of its own and that was anchored in our midst. People of various nationalities were on this pontoon, including some newspaper correspondents and some Chinese. Here the boldness of the British could be admired. The British gunboat pulled alongside the pontoon during the bombing, released its anchor chains and towed the pontoon to safety while bomb fragments were falling.

Two badly wounded Chinese were brought to our ship to receive first aid, but as we had no doctor on board we sent them to the American gunboat where they were treated.

I am no coward, but when you're on a tanker ship and hear the awful scream of shells falling, it truly makes you afraid!

The bombing had come as a complete surprise and we didn't even know who was bombing us. Only later we heard that it had been the Japanese. Bombing was occurring everywhere, especially in the cities.

At our new anchorage the entire night passed peacefully. Early the next morning we heard cannon fire, and around 8 a.m. shells began to fall ½-¾ mile below us, near the northern riverbank, amongst the Chinese junks there, and some of them were sunk.

Seeing that the situation was becoming worse, *Panay* signaled that we should heave anchor and follow her upriver. We passed the British ships that were anchored under the protection of two gunboats, and continued upriver.

When we were five miles upriver and near the northern riverbank, we heard rifle and machinegun fire. *Panay* was in the lead and we saw her stop above the island of Tedre and a motorboat filled with soldiers came alongside her. As we approached *Panay*, we saw Japanese soldiers on shore and we believed that the motorboat had also held Japanese soldiers. The Japanese soldiers stayed on *Panay*'s deck for about twenty minutes. Then they went back to shore and *Panay* continued sailing ahead, signaling to us that we should continue to follow her and that we were going to anchor 28 miles above Nanking. We reached this place at 10:30 a.m.

Mei Hsia was anchored near the northern riverbank, to our right, in line with *Panay* and in front of her. We were the furthest to the north but *Mei Hsia* was ahead of us. *Mei An* was closer to the southern riverbank and was almost parallel with *Panay*. We were comfortably anchored there and the small boats were tied to our ship.

After lunch, around 1:30 p.m., eight sailors from the American warship came onboard *Mei Ping* to get some food supplies. Having agreed to this, a radiogram from Shanghai to our manager was brought along from the warship, but this was in code and he couldn't understand it so I went to my cabin to get the codebook, took it to my manager in the saloon and then went to the bridge.

In the meantime, Japanese planes were flying over us from south to north at a very high altitude. They were hard to see but there were about twelve of them. We did not pay any attention to them as we were sure that the Japanese commanders knew where we were and that we were under protection.

Somewhat after 1:30 p.m., I heard a terrible explosion portside after which an American sailor shouted: "A bomb fell on *Panay* and *Panay* is sinking!"

I ran to the telegraph to get the engine ready while yelling for the anchor to be heaved. As soon as I received the response I sent the ship ahead on full steam.

Just as the ship had begun to move, I heard aircraft firing overhead and I instinctively flung myself down beside the compass. The steel shutters had already been lowered. Then I heard a horrible crack and everything around us shattered. The helmsman had also taken cover beside me.

When I got up, i saw that two bombs had fallen through the roof of my cabin, the steel door had been blown open and the cabin was in flames. The cabin no longer had a roof and we could also see that the sundeck had fallen down. I realized that the ship was damaged and it was necessary to take her ashore to the nearest place, the northern riverbank, about 100 fathoms away, to be able to save people should the ship sink. I heard the clatter of machineguns behind me as *Panay* was firing at the airplanes while she was sinking.

An American sailor yelled to me that a Japanese patrol coming downriver was firing its machineguns at the smaller boats, and all of our small motorboats and tugboats returned. I thought that if I put the ship onto the northern riverbank then the Japanese soldiers on the motorboats would likely shoot the people anyway, and it might be better to take the ship to the southern riverbank where a pontoon, belonging to a Japanese iron ore mine, would give people the chance to run ashore along the pontoon, as most Chinese did not know how to swim. If the oil were to ignite, though, then everyone would have to jump overboard and swim.

It was possible that the ship might sink before we reached the riverbank, but as there was no other avenue of escape I decided we should go to the southern riverbank and I turned the wheel in that direction. Then I heard another airplane diving and firing and I lay down again. I heard a crack and when I got up to look, I saw that a bomb had fallen about 10 feet away from the port side of the ship's bow. The ship did not seem to have any obvious damage, but we had no idea what shape she was in under the waterline.

The passengers came up from below. Our manager had been badly wounded. He had been below in the saloon when the bombs fell and he had many head wounds. The other American, the tobacco company manager, had hand and neck wounds. I asked them how they were feeling and they said that they only felt weak and were otherwise all right, so I asked them to go and help put out the fire and sent the helmsman along with them.

Another attack came and more bombs fell on the right side of the ship, but exactly where I didn't know. The lifeboats were destroyed, the steam pipe near the smokestack burst and the ship advanced very slowly. The Italian mechanic ran toward me to see if I was still alive, and if I had not been he would have taken over control of the ship. However, I was still on the bridge by myself, controlling the wheel and the mechanic ran back to put out the fire.

As we were a tanker ship, we had very good firefighting equipment, and hoses were everywhere, but bomb fragments had cut them so badly that it took a lot of sorting before we were able to gather enough hose to begin fighting the fire.

The fire extinguishers had been thrown from their brackets onto the deck and were leaking, covering the entire deck with their contents. This made fighting the fire very difficult, as the extinguishers had drained out and were not of any use, so we lowered pails over the railing and filled them with water to try and extinguish the fire.

Each time we heard the airplanes coming again and more bombs falling I flung myself down on my stomach. After each explosion I got up to see where the bomb had fallen. In the meantime, the ship went in whatever direction it wished to. The crew and the passengers were fighting the fire. We finally made it to the southern riverbank, slightly ahead of the pontoon, and I changed into reverse gear so we would come alongside it. Again, I heard an airplane coming but as the ship was already moving backwards, the bomb fell in the water, five feet away, sending a wave washing over the deck and bomb fragments everywhere. The people were amidships so no one was hurt. The ship was just alongside the pontoon when an American sailor ran ashore and another sailor gave him a cable, which he fastened, and then he received another cable. The bow of the ship was soon secured and I disengaged the engine. I yelled loudly for everyone to go ashore and I ran to the pontoon to help the women and children get off. The first people to run off the pontoon were met by Japanese soldiers brandishing bayonets, who gathered all of them into one group. After everyone else had left the ship, I also left and heard a Japanese officer asking for the captain. I presented myself, and the First Mechanic, and said that the ship belonged to Standard Oil, an American company, and that the crew and the other people were all employees of Standard Oil. They, however, insisted that it was a Chinese ship. Before I could reply, the Americans pointed to the American flag, which was still hanging from the mast, to confirm that the ship was American.

The fire aboard the ship was still burning and was growing in size, and while the Japanese began to search the Chinese we asked for permission to go back on board with the crew to fight the fire, and this was agreed to. We rushed back on board and after a half-hour of hard work we were able to get the fire under control.

Mei Hsia came near and, seeing us, asked about our situation and what I was planning to do. I replied that I was not leaving the wharf to go anywhere, that the ship had been almost impossible to steer, that the Japanese were in charge here and that our situation was unresolved. I asked what he thought and he said he didn't know, and would wait a bit to see what happened. Then I went ashore to see how the passengers were doing, and saw the Japanese giving first aid and bandaging those who had been injured. The Chinese however, were all in one group under guard, while the Americans were not watched so closely. We were thirteen white men but even we were not allowed to wander very far.

The Japanese tied one Chinese man to the railway tracks and planned to shoot him for being a spy. This man however, had been the driver of our car in Nanking and the pants of his work uniform happened to be similar in color to the uniforms worn by Chinese soldiers. The Japanese refused to believe that this man was a driver, even as I tried to explain to them that he had been our employee for sixteen years and that they should delay his execution and listen. They could arrest him if they wished but could not just immediately execute him. Eventually the Japanese agreed to wait.

Night began to fall and we thought that if Chinese forces were in the vicinity they might come to attack the Japanese and then we would also come under fire. I asked if we could go back to our ship, and the Japanese gave us permission to do so. While going back on board I saw that Mei Hsia had come alongside us and had not gone to the pontoon below. I asked the captain about this and he replied that the Japanese officer had insisted that he go beside Mei Ping. I then asked about the situation aboard his ship, and he replied that the ship was not damaged but that the first bomb had exploded very close to them. The crew had been on deck and because of this everyone except the helmsman and he had fallen over the rail. He had saved most of the men himself and the motorboats had picked up some of the others. He did not know how many had drowned.

Because the Japanese had not yet administered first aid to all of the wounded, especially to the Europeans, the medic from the American gunboat also began to give first aid, as the medical supply cabinet of Mei Hsia had remained intact while ours had been completely destroyed.

I ordered the crew to collect all the debris from the deck and to throw it overboard while I waited my turn to have my hand looked at. It had been so badly wrenched that I was unable to use it. I didn't know how this had happened, but my left hand was useless and I hadn't realized that I could not move it until starting to go back to the ship.

Suddenly, I received an order from the Japanese officer to come back ashore to discuss the situation of the driver from Nanking. Stepping off the ship onto the pontoon, I met a Japanese officer who held the rank of Major, and he spoke a little English. He asked if I would provide my guarantee that the man was simply a driver and not a soldier. I readily agreed to this and to do so in writing I went back to *Mei Hsia* because my cabin, clothing and belongings had all been destroyed.

The bombs had wounded my manager and the manager from the American tobacco company, Mr. Vines, who had been in the saloon when they heard the airplanes attacking.[14] Mr. Vines had immediately taken cover under a teak table. When a bomb fell onto my cabin, destroying it, bomb fragments had flown through the ceiling of the saloon completely breaking the table, but Mr. Vines had suffered only minor injuries to his right hand and his neck. Mr. Pickering, our manager, had no idea where he was or what had happened to him — his head was filled with glass shards and he thought that he had been near a window or a picture frame.[15] The others who were wounded had been on the deck.

Just as I was about to go back to the ship to write the guarantee, I heard an airplane diving and I quickly turned around to find a place to take cover. I threw myself down on my stomach near the wooden guard hut, with the Japanese Major slightly behind me and a Chinese, *Mei Hsia's* steward, between us.

Then the bomb fell, and then another, and right away I saw that they had both fallen onto *Mei Ping's* rear cabin, which contained 300 tons of gasoline that immediately exploded. The mast flew skyward in a flash of fire and the explosion caused a loud roar and released a torrent of fire in every direction. I yelled

---

14 F. Vines, was the Nanking manager for the British American Tobacco Company.
15 J.V. Pickering was Standard Oil's Nanking manager.

for the crew to run ashore while I helped those that I could, and when no one else was coming back I hurried toward shore. However, the Japanese on the wharf did not let us pass though. I pushed myself through the others and explained who I was, but even this did not help. Then I heard another airplane diving, and no longer caring about the patrol of Japanese soldiers, I began running toward land and everyone else ran with me, even the Japanese soldiers. At the first shed I came to, which contained piles of iron ore, I threw myself stomach first onto the ground in the furthest inside corner and the Chinese threw themselves down beside me, and on top of me, and wherever they happened to land.

I heard two explosions again. Looking up, I saw *Mei Hsia*'s mast fly up in the air and a flash of fire coming from her forward cargo room, which held gasoline. Then I saw that both ships were on fire - one at the front and the other at the rear. Hearing the airplanes diving again, I ran behind a nearby mound of iron ore and dropped onto my stomach. I heard the Japanese yelling and saw them waving their flags at the airplane so that it would stop shooting, but nothing helped. I heard crackling, first on one side and then on the other. Getting up I saw that one bomb had fallen between *Mei Hsia* and *Mei Ping*, or on *Mei Hsia*'s bow, and the other had fallen onto land amidst the Japanese, certainly killing some of them.

I turned back to see what had happened to the captain of the other ship and to the Europeans who had been onboard receiving first aid. They started coming toward me one at a time. Some of them were very badly wounded. The last one to appear from the side of the ship onto the pontoon was Captain Jørgensen and he was unhurt. I asked if anyone needing help was still on the ship. He said that everyone had already left, except for a few wounded who were being helped ashore by American sailors. I asked him if it was possible to save the ships. He replied that no one could save them now, and I had already been convinced of this. After the last people had reached land, I also left the pontoon and went ashore. The ships continued to blaze and the gasoline-filled iron drums aboard the ships ruptured and exploded one after another.

On our way back to the riverbank we saw that the Japanese had disappeared. They had taken their wounded and dead and had left in the direction of Nanking. The Chinese had wanted to follow, but the Japanese had pointed towards the woods — inland — and had not let anyone follow them.

When I stood up on the pontoon, I saw that the Chinese steward had been cut in half and that a Japanese officer had been heavily wounded — he died three days later.

Night was falling and as there was no shelter beside the river, we decided to go inland about 3 km. It was already dark by the time we arrived at an abandoned railway station, a narrow gauge railway that had been used to transport iron ore. Because some Chinese villages were nearby, we decided to stay there for the night.

The Americans thought that America and Japan were now at war, and they wanted to break through the Japanese lines to join the Chinese forces. They also thought that because the Japanese had sunk their ships, they also wanted to kill them for being witnesses to that.

I didn't support their thinking, though, as *Panay's* crew had remained on the other riverbank, as had *Mei An's* crew, and such an action would have created enough of a fracas without involving us. I also said it would be impossible to cross the Japanese lines with such a large herd of people, but they could do as they wished. I, however, would stay there because the easiest place to escape from was beside the river. A few of them wanted to proceed nonetheless, and some Americans ended up leaving. That night, not very far from there, they met a Japanese patrol and then came to the conclusion that getting through was impossible and they returned.

So we stayed — myself, Captain Jørgensen and Blasina, the Italian First Mechanic, to spend the night in an abandoned house with no doors or windows, along with the wounded Chinese.[16] The other Europeans sought shelter elsewhere. Because we were all lightly clothed, and also wet and dirty from the firefighting, it felt very cold with the wind constantly blowing through the structure. This was one of the worst nights, even though we had some rice straw that we had bought from the Chinese. Captain Jørgensen still had some money left in his pocket, but I had none. We lay down in the straw and tried to sleep but it was not possible. I was just drifting off when I heard bombs exploding in my imagination and saw accidents in front of my eyes, and thus I could not fall asleep.

Now that we were no longer on the ship we were overcome with a feeling of loneliness, like all had been lost. We were not afraid, but had somehow fallen out of line and no longer cared about anything.

I remember that when we were already ashore and another airplane began to attack, an American sailor said that *Panay* was sinking. When I looked, I saw *Panay's* stern still in the air and then she disappeared.

Six bombs had initially hit *Mei Ping* and the other three ships in the convoy, and another six bombs had fallen afterwards for a total of twelve bombs that had hit the ships. Our ship had a large smokestack that was filled with holes like a sieve. The lifeboats

---

16 Captain Birger Jørgensen's surname, like many European and Scandinavian names that originally contained accented letters, was often recorded phonetically as Jorgenson.

had been destroyed, but the steel had been strong enough that bomb fragments had not penetrated through to hit me. The bombs had blown doors off their hinges. The base of the compass had been blown askew, the steel plating had been bent, all the instruments had cracked open and the clock was in three pieces, each piece in a different corner. The searchlight and its frame had been ripped off of the bridge and tossed onto the deck.

A total of twenty-three people had been killed, two were lost, twenty people had been wounded, some of them very seriously, and one woman had a broken shoulder.

Four white people had been wounded, one of them badly, namely Mr. Marshall, the American correspondent, who stayed alive nonetheless. Two others were more lightly wounded and another one especially lightly.

One family comprising the father, mother, their ten children and a niece had all been killed in one attack, as had another family consisting of the parents and three children. On my ship, those killed included the Chinese First Mechanic, 4 machine greasers/ boiler stokers and the stevedore from Nanking.

On December 13th we gathered all the Europeans together and found that three of us were missing. We later received a message that they had gone to Wuhu, about 28 miles away. Two among them had been badly wounded but survived the trip. They had met a Japanese armored vehicle on their way, which had picked them up and taken them to Wuhu. From there, the wounded were taken to Shanghai by airplane. The rest of us, however, remained where we were. I made a plan for us to get out. The first night it wasn't bad, as the Chinese bandits did not know where we were and they were afraid of the Japanese, but later it became more dangerous. The others thought that we should go towards Wuhu but I suggested that we wait, because it was possible that people were coming to look for us. It was not possible to lose four American ships without anyone hearing about it.

In the meantime, we planned to send a letter to the Catholic priest in Wuhu asking for help. We wanted to send another letter to Japanese Army headquarters, which was inland about 20 km away. It was difficult to find someone who would deliver a letter to the Japanese. The Chinese did not want to go but were willing to go only a certain distance and no further. An American machinist said that he would go on the condition that some Chinese accompanied him as far as they would go and then waited for him there until he delivered the letter and returned. One Chinaman promised to take the letter to the Catholic priest for ten American dollars.

After we had finished our negotiations, a message came from the river, where we had placed a watch, that a British gunboat was coming downriver and approaching *Mei An* on the opposite bank. We thought that a few Europeans should go to the riverbank and try to send a signal. Our manager, who was wounded but not so badly that he couldn't walk, thought that he would go because then he would be able see a doctor sooner. Along with him went an American machinist who was going to do the signaling.

When they reached the riverbank, about two km away, the gunboat came toward our burning ships and stopped. Now we were certain that they had come to search for us, and that we were saved. We still feared that the Japanese might come to bomb us once they knew where we were, as airplanes flew over us night and day, although they had not bombed us here. We were not afraid of the Chinese soldiers but we feared the bandits who would take Europeans hostage and then demand large ransoms. We did not want to stay where we were any longer, not for even a single night, because we didn't have any weapons for protection.

The Chinese asked us not to go onto the ship and abandon

them, and this is why I decided not to leave before we received a message. Soon a senior British officer and doctor, an American mechanic and four British marines came from the gunboat to take us away.

The doctor began to look after the wounded. We gathered all the Europeans together and went towards the gunboat. The wounded Chinese remained behind, but the others came to the ship with the hope that maybe they would be taken onboard as well. However, that did not happen.

It was already dark, around 6 p.m., when we arrived aboard the HMS *Bee*. I felt that I was saved. The British officers gave me two large glasses of vermouth to drink. As I usually drank sparingly, I would normally have become drunk from this amount but I had been under such stress that I didn't feel a thing. I borrowed some money for my crew, and the manager borrowed some money for the other employees, from the British cashier. He then gave the money to the Chinese and promised that they would be looked after in the future, as much as this was possible. We left the wharf and sailed to the middle of the river to drop anchor. The ship used its radio to transmit the names and nationalities of those who had been picked up and I was on the list as well. Of the officers and crew who had remained on *Panay* however, we didn't know anything. Nor did we know anything about those on *Mei An*, other than she was staying five miles below us.

At around 10 p.m. on December 13th the first Japanese gunboats and one cruiser came and anchored beside us. The Japanese officers paid the British Admiral a visit, having come to see how things were. In the morning, we were informed that the British Admiral and others were going ashore to the north bank to search for survivors from *Panay*, and until it was known what had happened to her crew the ship would not leave.

We spoke with our manager about the need for the wounded Chinese to have their injuries treated. The Japanese offered help from their gunboat. I went to the south bank with the Japanese doctors to look for our wounded. As the motorboat had a machinegun mounted on it, we hoisted a white flag and waved this about so that no one from shore would fire at us.

We reached the bank and found only *Mei Hsia's* Chinese mechanic and one stoker. They came to meet us and said that no one else was there as they had returned inland to where we had previously stayed. We advised the Japanese that the wounded were inland and asked if they would come with us, but they categorically declined. I then asked if they would wait until we brought the wounded here. They replied that they would return to their ship to wait, and would return to the riverbank when they saw us coming with the wounded.

I tied my handkerchief on top of a stick as a white flag and we headed inland. When we arrived we gathered the Chinese together. The farmers said that the railway had a handcar and that up to six wounded people would fit on it, and they were kind enough to go and bring it there and so we used it to transport the wounded. After 1½ hours, all of them were on the riverbank and tending to them began. When the Japanese saw us from their ships they came to shore right away. Just about everyone needed medical attention, such as removing pieces of shrapnel, etc.

Three people were so badly wounded that nothing could be done for them. I sought permission to take them aboard the ship and then to Wuhu. The Japanese were initially against this but finally agreed to take them on board, although they did not want to take them to Wuhu. The others were to remain on shore, and when everything was ready we took the three badly wounded people back to the Japanese gunboat.

Just as the wounded were being bandaged, a Japanese

Admiral came by on a cruiser and began to bestow honor upon the British Admiral by way of a cannon-fire salute. This sent the Chinese into a panic as they believed the Japanese and the British were now at war and were starting to fire upon each other. They wanted to run away and our attempts at explaining did not help. When the firing stopped, however, and they saw that we were still on the riverbank then they dared to come back.

When the Japanese were giving us first aid, a Chinese priest came and tried to explain something to me. Because I could not understand what he was saying, his words were translated for me. He said that a wounded Chinese sailor from my crew was in his temple, about four km away. I asked them to bring this wounded man to the riverbank, which they kindly did. I asked how much they wanted in compensation for doing this and they categorically refused to accept any payment. This amazed me because the Buddha's priests wanted payment for every little service they bestowed. However, this time they wouldn't accept anything and were even sympathetic. It was the same with the farmers who had gladly helped us and wouldn't accept anything in return, but for their food they still demanded the price of blood. A pail filled with hot water cost two dollars, a bundle of straw cost five dollars, ten raw eggs cost three dollars, and a pail full of boiled rice, which at most was worth one dollar, cost five dollars. However, they couldn't really be blamed for this as they themselves had nothing to eat because everything had already been consumed.

After we arrived alongside the Japanese gunboat there was a lengthy discussion between the commander and the doctors before they took the three wounded people onto their ship.

I was taken back to the Admiral's ship, HMS *Bee*, where we heard that Holt, the British Admiral, had been in telephone contact with some *Panay* crewmembers who were inland in a

Chinese city, about twenty miles away, where there was a small hospital that had treated their wounded.

Of them, *Panay's* captain, Lieutenant-Commander Hughes, had been seriously wounded, with a broken hip and some other injuries. The First Lieutenant, the senior officer Anders, had badly injured hands and a bomb fragment in his throat. There were four dead, among them the Italian correspondent and the others were American sailors. There were eight seriously wounded men and others with more minor injuries.

At first these men did not want to come back at all, and demanded a guarantee that they would not be fired upon any more. The British Admiral gave this guarantee and they then promised to come to the riverbank by 10 p.m. and requested that some trucks be sent to come and get them.

The Japanese reported that they had boarded *Mei An* and found the bodies of a European and a Chinaman on the bridge but that no one else was on the ship, either dead or alive.

Then three Japanese seaplanes from Shanghai arrived and landed near us, bringing a doctor for medical assistance.

After lunch, at 2 p.m., the American gunboat *Oahu*, a sister ship to *Panay*, arrived from Hankow.

It was agreed with the Japanese that they would place the bodies of Carlson, *Mei An's* captain, and that of the Chinese man, into coffins and bring these to the American ship.

We then waited for nighttime, when *Panay's* crew was to reach the riverbank. Just before nightfall the British gunboat *Ladybird* arrived from Wuhu. The day before, the Japanese had opened fire on her from shore and had caused major damage to her deck. One man had been killed, the captain had been wounded and the Chief of Staff of the Yangtze River Fleet, who they wanted to take to Hankow, had received a hand wound.

The Captain of HMS *Ladybird* had dropped anchor and gone

ashore, at a place where it was not so easy for them to be shot at, to ask what was going on and why his ship was being fired upon. The Japanese replied that they had orders to shoot at all ships on the river.

I was invited to have dinner that evening with the Chief of Staff of the Yangtze River Fleet. He ate separately from the officers, usually with the Admiral. The British Army attaché from Nanking, who once had been in Estonia, was also there. He had been injured along with the British Ambassador, Sir Hughe Knatchbull-Hugessen, when Japanese planes had strafed the Ambassador's car on the same day that *Panay* had been sunk. The Ambassador later recovered, but was no longer able to fulfill his duties, and resigned. Also at dinner was the captain of the Japanese gunboat. I told them what had happened to us.

That night at around 1 o'clock in the morning, the wounded from *Panay* were brought from shore and taken immediately to the Admiral's ship, where they received treatment from Japanese, British and American doctors.

They had all suffered considerably coming overland and were in poor condition. They were dirty, having been in mud up to their necks, and going inland they had had to carry the wounded for long distances. Also, they had not been able to eat properly, were wet, and had been under a lot of stress.

The next morning notice was given that we were leaving for Shanghai that afternoon at two o'clock.

We were transferred to the American gunboat USS *Oahu*, to which the Japanese brought the bodies of a captain and a helmsman, both covered with Japanese naval flags. The bodies of two American sailors, who had been *Panay* crewmembers, and the body of the Italian newspaper correspondent,[17] were also

---

17   Sandro Sandri, correspondent for La Stampa of Turin

brought from shore.

We were advised that three Japanese cruisers would provide an escort to Shanghai. Before we left, the captain of the Japanese gunboat came and wanted to speak with me. He said that he was going to Wuhu and asked what should be done with the three Chinese who had been receiving medical care on their ship. I asked him to take the wounded to Wuhu and deliver them to a large hospital there. At first he did not want any part of this but in the end he nonetheless agreed to do as I requested. I gave him a very cold farewell and didn't even offer a handshake. The Japanese captain then asked me to wait and said that he was very sorry about the incident and wanted me to shake hands with him in reconciliation, which I finally did.

Already when I had been on shore with the Japanese giving aid to the wounded Chinese, I had informed them that I was Estonian. The head doctor had then asked me to give him my address in Estonia and I wrote "from Tallinn". The Japanese commander also knew my nationality and the Japanese knew where Estonia was, and even the common people knew. They know this better than the British and Americans.

When I went to say goodbye to the British Admiral even he knew that I was Estonian and he said that Estonians were good sailors. He had heard of Ahto Walter and some of his officers had even been to Tallinn after the Estonian War of Independence.[18]

On December 15th at 2 p.m. we headed downriver with *Ladybird* following us. There was one cruiser in front of us, one on our port side — where the riverbank was in Chinese hands — and one behind us. We sailed until we reached the British ships, where three ships filled with passengers joined us, and

---

18   Ahto Walter (1912-1991) was the first Estonian to sail around the world, in 1930, before immigrating to America. In 1932 he held the trans-Atlantic crossing record for 40 ft. sailboats.

continued until we were five miles above Nanking, where we anchored for the evening.

After we had anchored, Japanese motorboats brought sixteen Americans to our ship. They were the newspaper correspondents and missionaries who had been left behind in Nanking when *Panay* had fled.

We saw an incident where a Chinese log raft drifting downriver, with two Chinese on board, was passed by a Japanese motorboat. Then another Japanese motorboat came by and opened fire on the raft, wounding both of the Chinese, one of them badly. We sent a boat to help and brought them aboard the ship, where they were given medical attention, while their raft drifted onward.

At night the cruisers near us kept watch and fired their guns many times, shelling the Chinese on the northern riverbank.

The next morning, December 16th, we heaved anchor and continued downriver escorted by the cruisers. When we passed by Nanking in the early morning, the city was smoking and on fire, as was Pukow, and looking from the river there appeared to be little remaining other than rubble and ruins.

In the afternoon we reached the foreign ships, the British, Norwegian and American ships that had been standing there for four months already, unable to go downriver and waiting for the opportunity to exit the Yangtze. They joined us and we traveled together to the fort at Kiangyin where we again dropped anchor for the night.

The next morning two cruisers escorted us and we arrived in Shanghai at nightfall. When we were steaming into Shanghai there were already Japanese airplanes in the sky keeping watch to ensure that nothing happened to us on our way. The entire time all of the ships — the gunboats and our ships — had their flags at half-mast to signal that victim's bodies were aboard. We came beside an American cruiser named *Augusta* that was the flagship of America's Asiatic Fleet and carried the fleet Commander, where we were let ashore. The office manager was there to greet us and had brought some clothes and other necessities for us, as we had nothing and the weather was quite cold.

Before we were let ashore, an order came that the next morning at 9 o'clock we had to come and attest to our incident reports under oath. The reports had been given earlier to the *Oahu*'s captain.

The next morning after I had come aboard the cruiser USS *Augusta*, I was brought before a U.S. Naval Court of Inquiry, consisting of officers from American warships that were stationed in Shanghai. My incident report was read to me, corrections were made where necessary, and when everything was acceptable, I gave my oath that all of it was true.

A few days later, the badly wounded *Panay* boatswain died in a Shanghai hospital. The bomb fragment that had been lodged in Lt. Anders' throat, however, fell out into his throat on its own after three days and he recovered so well that there were no after effects and the wound healed rapidly. The initial assessment of Captain Hughes was that he would need to stay in hospital for 9 months and would be disabled for life.

On shore we began to deal with the payroll records of those who had been killed, those who were lost, those who had gone to Hankow — in general, dealing with the various affairs affecting the crewmembers of the Standard Oil ships. There were many people whom the office did not have any information about, i.e. whether they were still alive or not. These activities occupied me in Shanghai until the day of my departure, even though the term of my employment ended on December 31st with my final salary payment.

I did not visit the Hankow[19] section of town but about 60%-65% of it had been wrecked by the Japanese and the Chinese. The French Concession and International Settlement were still behind barricades of sandbags piled on streets and in front of windows. Some shooting was still heard, but not often.

The bomb damage to Nanking Road and Avenue Edward VII, however, had already been repaired and food supplies were plentiful again. There were an awful number of beggars, though, more than ever before, and there was also a lot of filth.

The Japanese did not venture out very much and when they did they were very cautious. They were rarely seen in the French Concession or in the International Settlement. One time five Japanese came to shore by motorboat and were attacked by the Chinese and beaten so badly that only three of them, with a lot of difficulty, managed to escape.

All Chinese-owned ships and tugboats in Shanghai sailed under foreign colors, either Greek, Norwegian, Swedish, German, British, American or others, as they had all been able to register the vessels in other nations. There were no Chinese flags.

The most senior Japanese military officer was Colonel Hashimoto, who happened to be in Wuhu. This was the same man who, several years before, was involved in an attempt to start a rebellion in Japan. He was a strong opponent of foreigners. We asked the Japanese for an explanation of why they had fired upon foreign vessels, and they replied that they had received a command from headquarters in Tokyo to sink all ships on the Yangtze River regardless of which flag they sailed under. In reality, Tokyo had issued an order that only Chinese ships were to be sunk while the Colonel insisted that his orders had been to sink all ships.

---

19   European

The Japanese then immediately issued an apology and promised restitution for all damages caused to foreign ships, as otherwise the Americans may have attacked them. The American people were very angry about this event.

Restitution was made in the total amount of U.S. $2,200,000. I recovered the cost of my clothing and other personal effects from my office, which received monies from the American government.

I had to write a list of how much my clothes were worth and what I had owned and finally I had to attest that my list was true by swearing an oath.

The American journalists questioned me about all of my experiences and those who had been onboard *Panay* had already written everything down. These notes were used for articles that appeared in American newspapers and I was also photographed and filmed — the film was to be shown in movie theatres.

12

LEAVING CHINA

On January 14th, 1938 I left Shanghai on *Contepagomono*, a large Italian passenger ship of 20,000-tons. I sailed on her to Hong Kong where I disembarked, as I wanted to visit there for a few days. I continued my journey on *Potsdam*, a German passenger ship, which took me to Genoa from where I went to my homeland by train. I arrived in Tallinn on February 12th. The journey had taken 26 days.

Traveling on the ships was lovely but my health was poor and I could not really enjoy the trip. What I had seen and survived had taken a toll on my health.

Having arrived home, I was happy to have escaped with my life. Death had been extremely close. I no longer had any desire to go back.

I consider myself fortunate to have found a good job in the Far East, one that paid a good salary — my employer was one of the largest companies in the world — on top of which we received an additional 40% when we were in the line of fire. The monthly salary of a captain there ranged from 250-600 Estonian kroons. Where did this come from?

Other Estonian mariners remained in China, including Captain P. Jakobson, who lives in the countryside, manages a guesthouse and occasionally goes to sea; Captain Leisberg, who sails a Chinese ship on the Yangtze River; Captain Kärner, who sails a Chinese freighter on the ocean; Captain Musikus, who sails on a British freighter on the ocean; and Captain Keskküla, who is living in the countryside. Some Latvian mariners also remained in China.

The number of Estonian captains in China has been declining over the years. At first there were seventeen captains, but now only five remain. They will likely all leave in the near future. Only a few of them have managed to accumulate any savings — those who were able to find good jobs and had continuous employment.

POSTSCRIPT

DESPITE LIVING in China for decades, Mender wasn't very comfortable living among the Chinese because he didn't really understand their culture. He was well paid and got along well with the Chinese, and they valued him, but he was unable to find a really good friend among them. Chinese men socialized with other men and their women with other women, and families never seemed to socialize together.

Some people stayed in China for 40-50 years, and those who were born there werre unaware of anything else and lived there quite contentedly, but those who moved there from somewhere else usually did not want to stay.

During the 30 years that Mender lived and worked in the Far East, he had only been back home three times on holiday, in 1924, 1930 and 1935. After his 1938 retirement from Standard Oil, he returned to his homeland for good, where he was able to buy a home in Tallinn that was large enough to have space for their married daughters and grandchildren.

While recovering from the stressful *Panay* incident that had taken place during the last few months of his employment, Mender decided to write his memoirs while his recollections remained clear. These were published 1940 in Tallinn. His manuscript was edited by another ship captain, Evald Past, who was also an author and had written close to half a dozen books about Estonian ships, captains and sailors. Both men were conscious of how quickly the shipping industry had changed since the days of sail and wished to preserve as much maritime history as possible for future generations.

Mender also became active with Merilaid & Co., the shipping company founded 1930 in Tallinn by Estonian captains returning from the Far East, along with relatives and others, where Mender was also a part-owner. One of his son-in-laws was also in the shipping business.

While Mender believed he had returned home to stay, events soon proved that good times do not last. Europe had never really settled down after the 1919 Paris peace talks that took place at the end of the First World War. By the mid-1930s trouble was brewing again. Germany and the Soviet Union secretly agreed to a mutual non-aggression treaty, the Molotov-Ribbentrop Pact, to divide some European countries between them.

In 1939, the Second World War began when Germany invaded Poland. In 1940, the Soviet Union invaded Estonia and other Baltic nations, executing or deporting anyone they believed to be a threat and nationalizing all industries including shipping companies. The husband of one of Mender's daughters was arrested and deported to a Siberian labor camp. Life was in turmoil again, similar to what Mender had lived through in China. People did not know what was going to happen next and fear and uncertainty prevailed.

In 1941, Germany violated their agreement with the Soviet Union and invaded the Baltics from the south, forcing the Russians to retreat. While people were pleased to see the Soviets forced out, life under German occupation was not much better. Britain had weathered German attacks and after America finally joined the war in late 1941, Hitler's fortunes began to wane.

As the war continued, it became clear that Estonia would no longer be independent and, despite not knowing which country would end up in control, some Estonians made plans to flee their homeland.

In 1943, with his maritime knowledge and connections, Mender and his family were able to flee by ship across the Baltic Sea to Sweden, just before the Soviets invaded Estonia for the second time. Russia had coveted access to the Atlantic Ocean since the days of Peter the Great and were determined to secure a Baltic foothold. As things turned out, at the end of World War II, in addition to having control over Estonia, Latvia and Lithuania, the Soviets got control of previously Polish territory that bordered the Baltic Sea at Kaliningrad

After reaching Sweden, Mender and his family, which included four grandchildren by then, considered their next move. While not at war with Sweden, the Soviets made threats against that country, demanding return of their "citizens" and assets (ships). Mender's employment with Standard Oil meant that he and his family were eligible for accelerated immigration to America, in significant priority to the otherwise several years-long waiting list, so Mender decided they would leave Sweden.

In 1944, Mender and his family migrated to America. He and his wife, along with two daughters and their families, ended up living in California, while his third daughter and her family remained in the east. Mender died in San Francisco in 1969.

The tremendous commercial growth in various industries – tobacco, oil, textiles, ship building, opium, shipping – that Mender witnessed in China's post-imperial to pre-World War II colonial era are unlikely to be repeated anywhere else, ever again. China's situation in the early 20th Century was unique not because the imperial dynasty fell, as this was happening in many nations, but because the land mass and population were enormous and, compared to western nations, the populace had little, if anything, in the way of modern infrastructure, manufacturing, transportation and consumer conveniences, meaning it was ripe for development. This was facilitated by the land and treaty port concessions to foreign nations. During the 1920s Shanghai was considered to be the Paris of Asia and the well-built modern buildings on the Bund in the French Concession, along with prosperous business people and large foreign companies, stood in sharp contract to the lives of ordinary Chinese.

The Yangtze River basin in this era quite possibly illustrated the height of colonialism, the great dichotomy between nations, and was something that Mender just stumbled upon while striving to provide for his family in the social milieu that was China in the early 20th century.

BIBLIOGRAPHY

Anderson, Irvine H. Jr., *The Standard-Vacuum Oil Company and United States East Asian Policy, 1933-1941*, Princeton University Press, 1975

China Imperial Maritime Customs, *Names of Places, China Coast And The Yangtze River*, Shanghai, 1904.

Cochran, Sherman, *Encountering Chinese Networks: Western, Japanese, and Chinese Corporations in China, 1880-1937*, University of California Press, 2000.

Grover, David H., *American Merchant Ships on the Yangtze, 1920-1941*, Praeger Publishers, Westport, CT, 1992. (Chap. 6 focuses on Standard Oil; Chap. 15 on pages 177-185 describes the *Panay* incident.

Grover, David H., *Yankee captains on the Yangtze river*, Western Maritime Press, Napa CA, 1995.

Grover, David H., *The Panay's Unknown Rescue Ship*, Sea Classics magazine, Vol. 29, No. 3, March 1996, pp. 14-19, 50-51, obtained from The Mariner's Museum Library in Newport News, Virginia.

Grover, David H., *Sparring with Dragons: Captain Giliberto - A Yangtze Legend*, Sea Classics Magazine, August 2008. (Gaetano Giliberto joined Standard Oil's Yangtze River fleet in 1928, beginning as chief mate on *Mei Ping*.)

Howland, Joseph E., *The sinking of the U.S.S. Panay*, Thesis (M.A.) Stanford University, 1948.

Hunt, Michael H., *Americans in the China Market: Economic*

Opportunities and Economic Nationalism, 1890s-1931, The Business History Review, Vol. 51, No. 3,(Autumn, 1977), pp. 277-307, See http://www.jstor.org/pss/3113634

McEndarfer, J., *The Chinese Bandit Menace in 1930*,Indiana University, 1998, http://www.iusb.edu/~journal/static/volumes/1998/Paper9.html - JodiMcEndarfer.

Morgan, V.L., *Exchanging Favors: The Fossil Hunter and the Yangtze Patrol, March 1923*, A working manuscript based on the records of Walter Granger, Chief Paleontologist of The American Museum of Natural History's Central Asiatic Expeditions to China and Mongolia during the 1920s.

Noble, Dennis L., *Gunboat on the Yangtze, The Diary of Captain Glenn F. Howell of the USS Palos, 1920 - 1921*, McFarland & Company, 2002.

North China Department, *The Mei Foo Shield*, monthly newsletter, various editions, obtained from the ExxonMobil Historical Collection held in the Briscoe Center of American History at the University of Texas at Austin.

Perry, Hamilton Darby, *The Panay Incident, Prelude to Pearl Harbor*, The Macmillan Company, 1969

Plant, S.C., *Handbook For The Guidance of Shipmasters On The Ichang-Chungking Section Of The Yangtze River*, Imperial Maritime Customs, Shanghai, 1920.

Perry, Hamilton Darby, *The Panay Incident, Prelude to Pearl Harbor*, The MacMillan Company, 1969.

Pugach, N.H., *Standard Oil and Petroleum Development in Early Republican China*,The Business History Review, Vo. 45, No. 3 (Winter 1971), pp. 452-473. See http://www.jstor.org/pss/3112809

Spencer, J. E., *Trade and Transshipment in the Yangtze Valley*, Geographical Review, Vol. 28, No. 1 (Jan. 1938), pp. 112-123, See http://www.jstor.org/pss/210570.

The Argus (Melbourne newspaper), *Bomb Attack on Gunboat,* December 15, 1937, http://newspapers.nla.gov.au/ndp/del/article/11132774;

The Straits Times (Singapore), *Skipper Sees Planes Sink His Ship,* January 30, 1938, The skipper is Mender. See http://newspapers.nl.sg/Digitised/Article/straitstimes19380130.2.21.aspx;

TIME Magazine reported on the conflict with Yang Sen in their September 20, 1926 edition, see http://www.time.com/time/magazine/article/0,9171,880893,00.html

Wilson, D.A., *Standard Oil Responds to Chinese Nationalism, 1925-1927,* Pacific Historical Review, Vol. 46, No. 4 (Nov. 1977), pp.625-647, See http://www.jstor.org/pss/3638166.

ACKNOWLEDGEMENTS

THANK YOU to the Briscoe Center of American History at the University of Texas at Austin, which houses the ExxonMobil Historical Collection. They kindly shared historical company newsletters such as The Mei Foo Shield, the Stanvac Meridian and the Mobil Mariner, which highlighted events in their Far Eastern operations over the years.

Thanks also to The Mariner's Museum Library in Newport News, Virginia for making available Samuel Cornell Plant's significant 1920 publication that documented the hazards of the Upper Yangtze River for the benefit of ship Masters undertaking this hazardous journey.

I'm blessed that my parents were able to help in translating parts of the book where Peter's idioms, vernacular and slang were outside of both my experience and the guidance that any dictionary could provide. Any parts of the translation that may be inaccurate, however, are solely my responsibility.

About The Author

Peter Mender, an Estonian, sailed in Far East waters, mostly along the Yangtze River, for more than thirty years. He was Standard Oil's longest-serving captain on the treacherous Upper Yangtze, and in 1937 during the Japanese attack on Nanking, Mender's ship, the Mei Ping, along with the American gunboat U.S.S. Panay, was bombed and sunk. Mender received a U.S. Navy Expeditionary Medal for his rescue work during the incident. He became a U.S. citizen and retired to California.

About The Translator

Hillar Kalmar, a retired businessman who lives in Vancouver, is a distant relative of the author. His grandfather, an Estonian ship master and Mender's first cousin, also lived in Vladivostok and Shanghai while working in the Far East.

Lightning Source UK Ltd.
Milton Keynes UK
UKHW041516120422
401453UK00001B/65